IBSEN AND THE THEATRE

THE GOTHAM LIBRARY
OF THE NEW YORK UNIVERSITY PRESS

The Gotham Library is a series of original works and critical studies published in paperback primarily for student use. The Gotham hardcover edition is primarily for use by libraries and the general reader. Devoted to significant works and major authors and to literary topics of enduring importance, Gotham Library texts offer the best in literature and criticism.

Comparative and Foreign Language Literature:
Robert J. Clements, Editor

Comparative and English Language Literature:
James W. Tuttleton, Editor

IBSEN AND THE THEATRE

The Dramatist in Production

edited by
Errol Durbach

New York University Press · New York *and* London

© Errol Durbach 1980

First Published in the United States of America 1980 by
NEW YORK UNIVERSITY PRESS

Library of Congress Cataloging in Publication Data

Main entry under title:
Ibsen and the theatre.
 (The Gotham library of the New York University Press)
  1. Ibsen, Henrik, 1828–1906—Criticism and
interpretation—Congresses. 2. Ibsen, Henrik,
1828–1906—Stage history—Congresses. I. Durbach,
Errol, 1941–
PT8895.I23   839.8′226   79–47995
ISBN 0–8147–1773–X

Manufactured in Great Britain

Contents

2142080

Acknowledgements

I should like to thank the Canada Council for conferring upon Ibsen the honorary status of Canadian citizenship for the purposes of funding the 'Ibsen and the Theatre' conference – and Ronald Bryden for corroborating this view of Ibsen in his witty banquet address; the Consul General of Norway in Vancouver, Mr Nils Axel Nissen, and Mrs Liv Nissen, for their interest and support; Mr Peter Haworth for his participation in the evening of dramatic readings from Ibsen; Michael Meyer, as consulting member in London for the conference committee; and those committee members on the faculty of the University of British Columbia – Andrew Parkin, Donald Soule, Marketa Goetz Stankiewicz – and especially Philip Moir, who administered the financial and other arrangements, and Jonathan Wisenthal who first conceived of the idea of the conference and who braved the various crises that attended its realisation.

E.D.

Notes on the Contributors

Errol Durbach (editor) is Associate Professor of English at the University of British Columbia, where he teaches Modern and Comparative Drama. He has published many articles on Ibsen, and is currently writing a book on Ibsen and Romanticism.

Martin Esslin was head of the Drama Department of the BBC, where he produced nearly all of Ibsen's major plays for radio. He is an influential drama critic whose *Theatre of the Absurd* is a seminal study of modern avant-garde drama, and his books on Brecht and Pinter are also very highly regarded. Recently appointed as a Professor of Drama at Stanford University, Martin Esslin now divides his time between London and California.

Inga-Stina Ewbank is the Hildred Carlile Professor of English at Bedford College, London, and is a well-known scholar of Renaissance drama, author of a book on the Brontës, and a distinguished Ibsenite. She has written several papers on Ibsen's language, translated *John Gabriel Borkman* for the National Theatre, *Pillars of the Community* for the Royal Shakespeare Company, and last year provided a literal translation of *Brand* on which the National Theatre's poetic version was based.

James McFarlane is Professor of European Literature at the University of East Anglia, Norwich, and is general editor of the *Oxford Ibsen* (London, 1960–77), published in eight volumes. He has published many books and articles on European and Scandinavian literature in general, and on Ibsen in particular. He is also editor of *Scandinavica: An International Journal of Scandinavian Studies*. He was elected Fellow of the Norwegian Academy in 1977.

Lise-Lone Marker, Professor of Theatrical History at the Graduate Centre for Study of Drama, University of Toronto, is the author of *David Belasco, Naturalism in the American Theatre* and other studies.

Frederick J. Marker is a Professor of English and Drama at the University of Toronto. His books include *Hans Christian Andersen and the Romantic Theatre, Kjeld Abell*, and several editions and translations. Together, the Markers have published a number of joint studies, including *The Scandinavian Theatre: A Short History*, and a portion of *The Revels History of Drama in English, 1750–1880*.

Michael Meyer, Fellow of the Royal Society of Literature and a Knight Commander of the Polar Star (Swedish), is the author of *Ibsen: A Biography* which is widely acclaimed as the definitive life of Ibsen, and winner of the Whitbread Biography Prize in 1971. He has translated all of Ibsen's major plays, and sixteen plays by Strindberg for which he received the Gold Medal of the Swedish Academy in 1964. He is also the author of a novel, and of several plays for radio, television and stage – his most recent, *Lunatic and Lover*, about Strindberg and his three wives, winning the Best New Play of the Fringe award at the 1978 Edinburgh Festival. At present, he is writing a biography of Strindberg.

John Northam, after thirty years at Clare College, Cambridge, moved to a Chair in the Department of Drama at Bristol in 1972. He is the author of *Ibsen's Dramatic Method*, a landmark in modern Ibsen studies, and he has recently published *Ibsen: A Critical Study*. As well as his many articles on Ibsen, Professor Northam's translations of some of Ibsen's poems have appeared in the *Ibsenårbok*.

Evert Sprinchorn is Professor of Drama at Vassar College, New York, and a well-known and influential critic of Scandinavian drama. He has published many articles on Ibsen and Strindberg, translated Strindberg, and is also the editor and translator of *Ibsen's Letters and Speeches*.

Janet Suzman's repertoire of dramatic roles extends from Shakespeare to Brecht and Athol Fugard, and she has appeared in many television and screen productions. As Masha in *The Three Sisters* she won the Plays and Players award for best performance by an actress, and her Hedda Gabler, both on television and at the Duke of York's, has been greatly admired.

1 Introduction

ERROL DURBACH

I

The papers in this collection were delivered (in varying degrees of formality and informality) at the 'Ibsen and the Theatre' conference, sponsored by the University of British Columbia in Vancouver in May 1978 to celebrate the 150th anniversary of Henrik Ibsen's birth. They are not, of course, the sum total of the conference proceedings, which included question-periods, seminars, a plenary session, and an evening of dramatic readings – but they represent the basic material for discussion and debate.

As the title of the collection suggests, the contributors have at least this in common: that they are all concerned with Ibsen as a writer for the *theatre*, approaching him in their individual capacities as scholars and critics of drama and performance – Michael Meyer as biographer, linking the intensely private concerns of the life to the objective presentation of dramatic theme; Inga-Stina Ewbank as cultural amphibian, inhabiting the divided and distinguished worlds of Scandinavia and England, literary criticism and practical collaboration with leading theatre companies on texts for performance; the Markers as theatre historians, with a clear sense of Ibsen's plays as specific productions within a 'chronicle' of Scandinavian tradition; Martin Esslin as director of Ibsen as radio-drama, and as comparatist, tracing lines of influence and genealogy from Ibsen to Brecht, Beckett and Pinter; Janet Suzman as actress, recreating Hedda's metamorphosis from text to stage from within the skin of the protagonist – the most detailed record of an Ibsen performance since Elizabeth Robins', fifty years ago; John Northam as linguistic analyst, concerned with the theatrical problem of modulating Ibsen's language from the prosaic chit-chat of the opening scene to the final poetic revelation of the protagonists' spiritual experience; Evert Sprinchorn as Professor of Drama and textual critic, comparing the complexity of Ibsen's plays to their treatment on the contemporary stage; and James McFarlane as translator, editor, anthologist, and critic – a veritable Lord High Everything Else of Ibsen scholarship – who sees the formal structure of an Ibsen play as a dynamic 'lattice-work' of constantly shifting relationships. A fear, voiced by Inga-Stina Ewbank, was that a group of Ibsen celebrants might all be inclined to give the same paper – a fear obviated by the variety of approaches that are evident in the essays.

It was not the intention of the conference committee to assemble a fully representative slate of contemporary approaches to Ibsen, or to evaluate the present state of Ibsen scholarship. There have been many uniquely valuable essays and books on Ibsen over the past five or six years dealing with his mythic patterns, his affinity with Hegelian ideas, his place in a modern existential and psychological tradition, and his treatment of the alienated hero; and in limiting our scope to text, performance and theatre we intend no exclusive assertion of method or approach. It remains remarkable that a dramatist writing in an archaic nineteenth century language – neither wholly Norwegian nor wholly Danish – and in a dramatic form that would seem to have fallen out of favour in the modern theatre, should continue to fascinate scholars from Canada to Japan and to hold his own on the stages of the world. It is this phenomenon that we wished to investigate, moved partly by the spirit of Ibsen's own address delivered in Christiania on the occasion of his seventieth birthday: his amazement at having won international recognition as a dramatist, and his delight at the friendship and understanding of foreign admirers; the rather melancholy awareness of the exile, who has won a home in strange lands, of his own essential homelessness, his 'alienness' (to borrow Inga-Stina Ewbank's term); and, especially, his sense of what is appropriate to an anniversary celebration – a gathering of divergent opinions and views around a single purpose. All I can hope to do, by way of introduction, is to provide a brief sampling of some such divergent opinions and then to suggest the singleness of purpose and the common concerns that underlie the eclecticism of this collection.

II

It is primarily in question and discussion sessions that differences and divergences are most fully aired – that procedure of thrust and parry, of statement and response, on which the relevance and reputation of a controversial dramatist thrive. Failing a full (and, surely, undesirable) report of the complete proceedings of the conference, a volume like this can only imply – by juxtaposition and concealed internal debate among the individual contributions – some of the more notable oppositions: Ibsen our contemporary, and Ibsen the Victorian; the Anglo-American Ibsen, and that other 'alien' Ibsen; the triumph of Ibsen on the modern stage, and the failure of modern Ibsen productions; the revelation of dramatic meaning through the sensibility of the central protagonist, and the meaning that derives only from the fields of force existing among all the characters in the play; Ibsen on the stage, and Ibsen on the page. As a paradigm of divergent opinions – which does not necessarily imply contradiction or radical opposition – I offer an edited discussion of a topic that arose at the concluding forum, the mythological relevance of the 'vine-leaves in the hair' motif in *Hedda Gabler*.

Chairman: Janet Suzman has suggested that the vine-leaves are not really mythological, but a private joke that Hedda shared with Løvborg which was re-invoked when they met again. Can you comment on that?

Janet Suzman: We know what the picture of a young man with a wreath of vine-leaves in his hair conjures up for us and so we've no need to explain it, really. Hedda might have gathered some small amount of knowledge about this young Bacchus creature from old pictures or statues – but even if she didn't know his name, he would have entered her imagination as a very powerful, beautiful image. I imagined that there was a lot of in-talk between Eilert and Hedda in their younger days, and in private. And when you talk with great friends you invent a language of your own which, when you are grown up, seems silly – because it's out of context, and therefore has lost that delicious secrecy it used to have. It is for *us*, with our tremendous historical knowledge, to receive that image – but I felt that for Hedda and Eilert it was a private, almost adolescent language which they might have laughed about a great deal. . . . And then, of course, it dies completely in her final scene with Eilert. She is grown up now – I mean that in relation to her adolescent secret. She doesn't believe in the vine-leaves any more. They obviously no longer have that reverberation that they used to have.

Michael Meyer: I've always felt a bit differently about those vine-leaves, not necessarily rightly – but I've always thought of them as the expression of Hedda's idealised and totally unrealistic view of men. Hedda's always seemed to me the kind of girl who has a dream vision of men as a band of heroes, superbly muscled, dressed only in G-strings, who descend and save you from the rock on which you're chained, with a dragon breathing fire at your feet – but who cannot bear to be touched by any man . . . because when he puts his hand on you (as Løvborg did) he ceases to be a dream man and becomes the man who wants you.

When Ingmar Bergman did this production in London, he cut one-sixth of the play and among other things, to Maggie Smith's horror, he cut all references to the vine-leaves – because he thought they were boring. I've always been doubtful about the vine-leaves – I've often felt they jarred a bit in productions I've worked on – but, taken away, the text and the play lost tremendously by their absence.

Chairman: One point the Markers made was that Ibsen emerges from a Victorian theatrical tradition. The Hedda who speaks about vine-leaves is at least vaguely familiar, I suppose, with Nietzschean ideas – even if she hasn't read *The Birth of Tragedy* she has at least absorbed something of its ideas from the cultural climate. How do *you* see the vine-leaves?

F. J. Marker: It won't have escaped the notice of those who know the original language that Løvborg's surname gives you a rather demythologised way of looking at the vine-leaves. Løvborg means 'leafy castle'.

Janet Suzman: It's wonderful. But I can't *act* it. You see how it is necessary for *me*, at any rate, to personalise a grandiose image.

Chairman: But there *are* ways of acting it. One can simply act it as Romantic nonsense, or one can choose to embody that idea in the search of a woman for a demi-god in a society that does not contain them.

James McFarlane: Hedda's reference to vine-leaves in the hair is not the first in Ibsen. There is another reference in *Emperor and Galilean*, an historical play dealing directly with the conflict between the Christian ethic and the Pagan ethic in fourth century Byzantium. Here the vine-leaves in the hair obviously refers to the old Greek paganism, to the Dionysian view of life – which, incidentally, is also linked, through repeated references, to *beauty* as distinct from *duty* (which is the Christian ethic). And so a kind of polarity is set up in *Emperor and Galilean* where the Christian virtues of love, meekness, submission, and so on exist in one category; and in the other category you have vigour, loyalty, a robust conscience, initiative, and those virtues that were thought of as belonging to the pagan view of life. I always respond, when I see *Hedda Gabler* or read it, to the vine-leaves as representing Hedda's desire for a kind of old paganism and beauty, an emphasis on doing something beautifully, doing it ruthlessly, doing it with courage, with an emphasis on loyalty between comrades.

If one takes it further than this, one then arrives at something that Martin Esslin made reference to: Ibsen's role as a factor in the cultural history of the last one hundred years. We should not leave out of account the fact that Ibsen *does* have a study life, *does* have a life on the page – a cultural factor of enormous significance. He is someone who took up and gave dramatic expression to an event at the end of the nineteenth century, which is probably the decisive thing that happened to our Western culture in the last one hundred years: the decline of the Christian ethic, and the attention given to a new kind of paganism.

F. J. Marker: As interesting as all these very specific references to Nietzsche and to mythology and the other cultural phenomena may be, I would merely want to suggest that perhaps some of these symbols are more 'unattached' and less directly representational of this, that, or the other thing. . . . The fear that dramatists like Beckett and Pinter have to the kind of thing being done to the vine-leaves is a very real fear, shared by producers like Bergman; and it is this fear that prompts Bergman to remove something like the portrait of General Gabler or the vine-leaves – which have tended to give this sort of academic, representational, literary, tied-down quality to an image which is more resonant and 'free-floating'.

Inga-Stina Ewbank: I think there is really no contradiction between the very eloquent protestations from both sides. Obviously I would have thought the actress playing Hedda must make the vine-leaves part of *her* language – *she* knows what it means. What Bergman is reacting against is that kind of tradition where the actress has been made very pretentiously to feel that she is pronouncing a 'symbol' – and so the thing is deadly and ominous. As an *audience*, surely the first time we hear of vine-leaves we think this a little odd; on the second occasion, we already hear it as an echo; and so on. And we begin, willy-nilly, to perceive each of those moments as typifying Hedda – but Hedda in a *context*, a comment *on* Hedda being delivered as well. When Macbeth speaks of pity like a 'naked newborn babe' we are bound to remember that other babe that Lady Macbeth tore from her breast and crushed against the stones. And we feel differently about the image. We don't feel that this is just the inside of Macbeth's mind (although it *is* that too), but we have a comment given us *on* Macbeth. This is where we can meet on the matter of the vine-leaves.

F. J. Marker: It is interesting what you say. But so often our references go back to Shakespeare or to English analogues, rather than to those that are much more germane to Ibsen himself – namely the Scandinavian analogues. What would occur to a Scandinavian audience hearing 'vine-leaves' repeated is something which is difficult to explain to North American students: the laurel crown with which every great artist, playwright, and actor is crowned in the Scandinavian theatre; and that crowning with vine-leaves has a very specific theatrical resonance which would be picked up by a Scandinavian audience, but not by an English or North American one – although there are *other* resonances that would be picked up.

Inga-Stina Ewbank: I wasn't really talking of the *substance* of the image, but the *form* to which an audience would respond, recognising it as a repetition and thinking, 'Here is something much larger than the individual. Here's a comment on the individual from the *outside*.' Then, I couldn't agree more that the *substance* of that comment could mean very different things: a doctoral procession in Lund or Oslo, or a reminder of Nietzsche's *The Birth of Tragedy*.

This multiplicity of possibilities, divergent views, and equivocal truths that cling to so many of Ibsen's images, themes, and ideas have much to do with the fascination of his plays and to their continuing dramatic vitality. The kaleidoscopic quality of his drama that Muriel Bradbrook senses in *The Wild Duck* is surely inherent in all Ibsen's plays. ' "The single vision" ', she writes, 'deepened and grew mysteriously active, mutable and various; the tide rises and falls, the light fades and gleams; to seek definitions is to go and catch a falling star. One day it will read as a tragedy, the next as harshest irony; parts of it are clumsy, in other parts are embedded old controversies of the time. So searching yet so delicate is the touch, that those flaws and vagaries seem in themselves to strengthen the work.'[1]

To reconcile these contradictions and oppositions and divergences into some Third Empire of academic criticism is to create that dangerous condition of deadly stasis which Ibsen's own seekers after synthesis, absolute truth, and ultimate meaning inevitably suffer in their own bitter experience.

III

After a century of Ibsen criticism it is not perhaps surprising that so many different approaches have been defined and explored. What is more surprising is that so much information still *needs* definition and exploration – especially for the Anglo-American scholar or theatregoer. 'Ibsen's language', one of my colleagues has remarked, 'still sounds to me like words spoken through a blanket.' And this sense, in the English speaking world, of the 'muffled' quality of Ibsen's language, what Yeats complains of as the stale odour of Ibsen's spilt poetry, remains a point of dissension when Ibsen's greatness is evaluated – as Ronald Gray in *Ibsen: A Dissenting View* maintains. But, unlike James Joyce and Thomas Mann (both of whom, as Michael Meyer points out, learned Norwegian in order to read Ibsen) Yeats's judgment of Ibsen's poetry was not informed by any knowledge of the original text or of Ibsen's anomalous poetics – very different, obviously, from his own. The problem of Ibsen's dramatic language is one of the central issues that many of the papers in this collection engage – from the innuendo and nuances within particular words, to the peculiar linguisitic structure of Ibsen's Riksmaal, to the delicate gradations of language from the colloquial through biblical echoes to the poetry of ecstatic revelation, to the inextricable location of language within the structural framework of the play. I want, briefly, to suggest one possible direction in which these papers point us for the 151st year of Ibsen criticism.

The initial approaches by the actress to the text indicated by
Janet Suzman – 'feeling' the rhythms and tonalities of the original,
the subtextual undertones, the precise notations of names and forms
of address, the degree of euphemistic implication in essentially
untranslatable words – all suggest an extraordinary degree of
scrupulous 'homework'. Miss Suzman's anecdote about the search
for a word to describe the exact anatomical region of Løvborg's
wound may be amusing, but it leads to the heart of the dilemma:
how to convey, even approximately, the *risqué* quality of an
anachronistic term (presumably taboo in good 1890s society)
without descending to an inappropriate vulgarity. 'Stomach',
'abdomen', or 'groin' are the vague periphrases with which for
decades we have had to be content – I think Michael Meyer was the
first translator to annotate his translation of *underlivet*, and to reveal
the unrevealable:

> When Brack tells Hedda where Løvborg has shot himself, he must
> make it clear to her that the bullet destroyed his sexual organs;
> otherwise Hedda's reactions make no sense. To translate this as
> 'belly' or 'bowels' is again to miss the point, yet Brack must not
> use the phrase 'sexual organs' directly; he is far too subtle a
> campaigner to speak so bluntly to a lady.[2]

The reference to *underlivet* may, indeed, generate as many different
responses as the 'vine-leaves in the hair'. But to miss the *quality* of the
word is to remain impervious to one of the play's shocking ironies:
the ridiculous travesty of Hedda's orgastic demi-God, who destroys
his own sexuality. What remains after the ruination of pagan virility
(at any rate, as Hedda envisions it) is the playboy attitude of
Brack – the triumph of bourgeois sensuality. Self-destructing God-
head, *Götterdämmerung*, is an essential part of the play's structure –
which may be too ponderous a concept to rear upon one small
word; but translate *underlivet* as 'bowels' and you lose all resonance,
all the complexity of Ibsen's finely-crafted concepts.

How many other such concepts elude translation? And how do
we *know*, as English readers and theatregoers, what still remains *to be
known*? Trained though we are to detect the importance of veiled
biblical allusion in Beckett, how can we detect Ibsen's incorpor-
ation of phrases adapted from the Norwegian bible – translation
into dramatic idiom of phrases already 'translated' from a prior
source? And without such information can we trust our own

responses to the text? To read *Rosmersholm* in ignorance of its powerful biblical echoes is surely analogous to reading *Waiting for Godot* stripped (if one could imagine such a reading) of the substratum of Christian mythology which defines its structure, its theology, its dramatic pairings and juxtapositions.[3] Ansten Anstensen, over forty years ago, discussed these allusions where they are most obvious and dense – in *Brand* and *Peer Gynt* – but his comments on the later plays, where the allusions are submerged in the prose of colloquial speech, only touch upon the resonances of the text.[4] John Northam, here and elsewhere, has been an invaluable guide to the non-Norwegian reader; but his appeal for an annotated edition, to explain what is inevitably lost in translation, is one that still needs to be responded to if we are to give Ibsen's plays the degree of attention they demand.[5]

And even beyond the problems of connotation and allusion, there remains the structure of Ibsen's words, their etymology, their ineffable flavour, and the sensibility – so elusive of English equivalence – which they evoke: the 'otherness', the 'alienness' which has been Inga-Stina Ewbank's primary concern at this and other conferences. (Her annotated editions of *John Gabriel Borkman* and *Brand* for the National Theatre, and *Pillars of the Community* for the Royal Shakespeare Company exist, tantalisingly, in the limbo of unpublished manuscripts.) Compare, for example, these randomly chosen translations of Mrs Alving's famous utterance in *Ghosts* to the original:

'*Og så er vi så gudsjammerlig lysrædde allesammen.*'
(a) 'Ah! if we only had the courage to sweep them all out and let in the light!'
(b) 'And we are so miserably, damnably light-fearing, the whole lot of us.'
(c) 'And we are, all of us, so pitifully afraid of the light.'

If none of these is entirely satisfactory, then a word-for-word translation would clearly be no better: 'And so are we so god-sorrowfully light-frightened, all of us' – which sounds like very poor Hopkins, or Dylan Thomas. Little wonder that (a) seeks refuge in paraphrase (which, quite uncharacteristically, expresses the desire for heroism and light, despite Mrs Alving's chronic inability to enact the exorcism here described). Translation (b) not only *sounds* translated, but converts the tears of God – His pity and compassion – into their antithesis ('damnably'), linked together with a 'miserably' which, in context, transforms Mrs Alving's self-pity into a harsh value judgment. And (c), surely the most accurate in a dictionary sense, translates the specific and concrete implications of '*gudsjammerlig*' into an abstraction which loses all contact with the original etymology. '*Lysrædde*' in translation (b) retains its strong compound quality, undiluted by the monosyllables which inundate English prose – but I have the sense that Ibsen is *coining* a concept here, inventing a term for the inversion of a child's fear of the dark into an adult's fear of the light and the horrors it may (and in this play *does*) reveal. The concentrated ironies of Ibsen's poem 'Lysrædd' (*ca.* 1855) seem to inform the word with a power that eludes all translation 'after Babel'. The loss is ultimately incalculable. One consolation (to adapt a point made by James McFarlane) is that in *performance*, in our grasp of the entire architectonic structure of the play, meaning can be restored to language – as that awful and relentless sunrise in *Ghosts* shapes our perception of Mrs Alving's '*lysræd*' even as her words fail to articulate its ultimate horror. And another (peculiarly 'Ibsenian') consolation is implicit in all the papers that deal with his poetry: in confronting us with the reality of poetic loss in English translation, they also alert us to the essentially provisional nature of the judgments we, as non-Norwegian readers, make on Ibsen's texts.

One other point on which so many of the papers, in their different approaches, converge is the problem of Ibsen's realism – so often defined, now, as the quintessence of 'Ibsenism' in the most pejorative sense of that term, and employed as powerful evidence against Ibsen in dissenting arguments. 'Well-made', 'life-like', 'realistic' (inevitably qualified by epithets such as 'dowdy' or 'artificial') – these have all become terms critically abusive of the 'creaking machinery' of Ibsen's drama. And while assessments of Ibsen in this 150th anniversary of his birth often declare his themes to be vitally alive, they also declare his techniques hopelessly dead. Michael Billington (by no means a dissenter) sums up this prevailing view: 'My impression is that there is scarcely a dramatist of stature anywhere, under the age of 40, who would profess to be an Ibsenite, technically: equally there is scarcely anyone under 40 who hasn't been influenced by him thematically'.[6] 'Was-drama', he declares, 'has been replaced by Is-drama' – a fact of dramatic history also convincingly detailed by Martin Esslin in his essay. At the risk of appearing reactionary, I would question whether this shift in emphasis from Ibsen's theatre of realism and gradual revelation to that of the neo-Brechtian parable has not *reduced* the nature of modern drama from the complex to a simplified vision of human experience.

Arthur Miller, a self-declared apologist of Ibsenism, makes no such radical disjunction between realism as an Ibsenist technique and realism as a way of perceiving the world. Being over the age of forty might, in Michael Billington's terms, disqualify him from consideration here; but he surely represents a dramatic tradition in which realism, in all its Ibsenist guises, is still predominant. (Is there a major American play, from *The Iceman Cometh* to *Who's Afraid of Virginia Woolf* – all permeated with the fear of living life without illusions – which is *not* a variation on the dialectical argument of *The Wild Duck*?) 'Was-drama' for Arthur Miller is the most distinctive and indispensable feature of Ibsenism: a *moral* vision of past actions and their consequences, a means of finding viable connections between past and future, and the dramatisation through this technique of evolving states of consciousness. Process, change, the 'wholeness' of the present as a moment in the flow of time, the profoundly dynamic aspects of 'Was-drama' – all these qualities argue against the view of technical Ibsenism as wooden or static or artificial; and the technique is ultimately inseparable from the vision of life, in all its myserious complexity, that Miller discerns in Ibsen's realism:

> This is the 'real' in Ibsen's realism for me, for he was, after all, as much a mystic as a realist. Which is simply to say that while there are mysteries in life which no amount of analyzing will reduce to reason, it is perfectly realistic to admit that . . . hiatus as a truth. But the problem is not to make complex what is essentially explainable; it is to make understandable what is complex without distorting and oversimplifying what cannot be explained.[7]

For Georg Lukács, as for Miller, the movement towards impressionism and naturalism has led to a narrowing vision, a levelling-down of the historical, social, moral being of man; and the aesthetics of realism – the presentation of complexity and completeness in human affairs – have been impoverished for him in the essentially reductive nature of modern alternatives to realism:

> True great realism thus depicts man and society as complete

entities, instead of showing merely one or the other of their aspects. Measured by this criterion, artistic trends determined by either exclusive introspection or exclusive extraversion equally impoverish and distort reality. Thus realism means a three-dimensionality, an all-roundness, that endows with independent life characters and human relationships.[8]

The greatest exponents of this form of realism in the late nineteenth century, writes Lukács, were the Russians and the Scandinavians. And it is appropriate to note, while celebrating Ibsen's 150th anniversary, that 1978 also marks the 150th anniversary of the birth of that greatest of all realists – Tolstoy – whose realism has, happily, never proved a source of embarrassment to his celebrants.

I do not want to suggest that any of the papers in this volume are polemical or apologetic in dealing with Ibsen's realism – but rather that they provide, even if unintentionally, a collection of perspectives on a moot point. No one would deny that some of Ibsen's devices 'clump across the stage,/As obvious as wigs'[9] – the coffin-ships, for example (very like the aircraft, with their cracked cylinder-heads, in Miller's *All My Sons*). But this is to take an extremely narrow view of the range of Ibsen's realism, its evolution and development, its experimental bases, and its extraordinary challenge to the modern stage. To share the Markers' historical sense of Scandinavian production from Bloch to Bergman, the directors' perennial quest for appropriate theatrical forms to accommodate Ibsen's vision, is to avoid the glib assumptions that still cling to the notion of Ibsen as technically effete. Moreover, after a decade of almost exclusive concentration in the theatre on the obviously well-made 'Was-drama' of Ibsen's *realistic* plays, attention is being redirected to the less obviously well-made *poetic* plays of the later period – only to reveal, as in James McFarlane's discussion of *Little Eyolf*, a latticework so finely crafted, so intricate, complex, and convoluting as to subvert entirely the clichés that obscure our sense of how well-made drama functions. And even the earlier plays, often condescendingly tolerated for their polemical ideas, are here shown to reveal the profundity of conception that Lukács recognises as the hallmark of Realism proper: the unfolding of all the possibilities – social and psychological – latent in humankind, the extreme presentation of extremes, and the revelation of the peaks and limitations of men and epochs. To give Evert Sprinchorn's Nora the vote, or Janet Suzman's Hedda the directorship of a bank would be as impertinent to their concerns as to lodge King Lear in a home for the aged. Stripped of those negative associations that blur our sense of Ibsen's realism, his drama moves towards that dimension of reality which Martin Esslin so eloquently defines in the closing paragraphs of his essay, and which will ensure his relevance for at least another 150 years.

NOTES

1. Muriel Bradbrook, *Ibsen the Norwegian* (London, 1946), p. 98.
2. *Hedda Gabler* (London, 1962), p. 117.
3. John Northam discussed some of these echoes in the question period following his paper.
4. Ansten Anstensen, *The Proverb in Ibsen* (New York, 1936).
5. Cf. John Northam, 'On a firm foundation – the translation of Ibsen's prose', a paper delivered at Cambridge in November 1976 as the Judith Wilson Lecture.
6. Michael Billington, 'The Ghosts in the Machine', *Guardian* (overseas edition), 2 April 1978, p. 20.
7. Arthur Miller, 'Introduction', *Arthur Miller's Collected Plays*, reprinted in J. W. McFarlane (ed.), *Discussions of Henrik Ibsen* (Boston, 1962), p. 105.
8. Georg Lukács, *Studies in European Realism* (1948), from Richard Ellmann and Charles Feidelson (eds), *The Modern Tradition* (New York, 1965), p. 351. See also Charles Lyons' definition of Ibsen's realism in *Henrik Ibsen: The Divided Consciousness* (Carbondale and Edwardsville, 1972), and his discussion of (and response to) Lukács' reservations about Ibsen's relationship to realism.
9. Roy Fuller, 'Ibsen', reprinted in J. W. McFarlane (ed.), *Henrik Ibsen* (Harmondsworth, 1970), p. 272.

2 Ibsen: a Biographical Approach*

MICHAEL MEYER

Some innovations are so seemingly basic that it is difficult to imagine a time when they did not exist, like fire and the wheel. Ibsen's contributions to drama are of this order. In brief, he was the first man to write a great tragedy in ordinary everyday prose, and the first to write a great tragedy about people called Mr and Mrs. Much besides, but consider these first.

When Ibsen wrote his first play in 1849, it was an accepted principle that stage tragedy had to be in verse. Prose was all right for comedy. You wrote *The School for Scandal* in prose, and the Falstaff and gravedigger scenes. But tragedy had to be in verse, like the earth going round the sun. People had tried to write tragedies in prose, especially in Germany during the previous hundred years, but none of these had quite come off and this seemed to confirm the rule. There had in fact been one exception; in the eighteen-thirties, Georg Büchner, before he died of typhus at the age of twenty-three, had written two magnificient tragedies in prose, *Woyzeck* and *Danton's Death*. But nobody knew about these; the manuscript of *Woyzeck* was not discovered until 1879, the year in which Ibsen wrote *A Doll's House*, and *Danton's Death* had been published only in a very corrupt version. And splendid as these plays are, they are written in a high-flown prose very close to poetry, like *The Playboy of the Western World*. But *Ghosts*, in 1881, was the first indisputably great tragedy written in ordinary everyday prose, and the importance of this for the future of drama can scarcely be exaggerated.

* Some of the matter in this talk has appeared in my biography of Ibsen (Hart-Davis, 1967–71). I am grateful to the publisher for allowing me to reprint it.

Likewise, *Ghosts* was the first great tragedy (again, excepting Büchner) about ordinary middle-class people. Before Ibsen, stage tragedy was about kings and queens or princes and princesses, or at the lowest Montagues and Capulets. When Ibsen's plays began belatedly to be performed in London in the eighteen-nineties, the drama critic of the *Daily Telegraph*, W. L. Courtney (who had been educated at Winchester and New College, a combination that few men survive), complained that they were:

> singularly mean, commonplace, parochial . . . as if Apollo, who once entered the house of Admetus, were now told to take up his habitation in a back parlour in South Hampstead. There may be tragedies in South Hampstead, although experience does not consistently testify to the fact; but, at all events from the historical and traditional standpoint, tragedy is more likely to concern itself with Glamis Castle, Melrose Abbey, Carisbrooke or even Carlton House Terrace.

In other words, as William Archer commented, Ibsen's characters were not what the Victorians called carriage people. Ibsen, in *Ghosts* and the plays which followed, showed that high tragedy could take place at least as easily and frequently in back-parlours as in castles and palaces, and probably more frequently, since there are more back-parlours than palaces. He wasn't of course the first dramatist to attempt this, any more than the Wright brothers were the first men to build an aeroplane. They were the first to build an aeroplane that got off the ground, and *Ghosts* is, after *Woyzeck*, the first tragedy about back-parlour people that gets off the ground.

Ibsen's third great contribution to the drama was technical. He threw out the old artificialities of plot which are usually associated with the name of Eugène Scribe, but of which Shakespeare and Schiller were also guilty: mistaken identities, overheard conversations, intercepted letters, and the like. It was a slow and painful process for Ibsen to rid himself of these; something of the old machinery is still there as late as *A Doll's House*; but his last ten plays are free of it. And, as A. B. Walkley noted as early as 1891, 'Whatever we learn, we learn at first-hand from the characters themselves, not from a Dumasian commentator or *raisonneur*.' Equally importantly, he developed the art of prose dialogue to a degree of refinement which has never been surpassed; in particular, that double-density dialogue which is his peculiar legacy, the subtext, the meaning behind the meaning. Through this he was able to create characters as complex as the most complex characters of Flaubert and Henry James. And this demanded, and opened the way for, a new kind of acting, analytical, self-effacing and sensitive (the kind most famously exemplified in his time by Stanislavsky and Duse). There was no place in Ibsen's plays for the old operatics.

None of these technical contributions explains the continued and ever-increasing life of Ibsen's plays on the stage today. Nobody outside a university puts on a play because of its historical importance. They live for the only reason that any serious play lives, because of the depth and subtlety of the writer's understanding of human character and (which is rarer) of human relationships; and because of his mastery of narration and plot. How many readers or theatre-goers, at the start of the final act of any Ibsen play, could, if they did not know it, predict the outcome? And yet when it comes, how inevitable that outcome always seems. A Swedish critic, Martin Lamm, has remarked of Ibsen that he is the Rome of modern drama. Ultimately, all roads lead from him and to him.

Ibsen was born in 1828, the same year as Tolstoy, in the little Norwegian timber port of Skien, a hundred miles south of the capital, Christiania (now Oslo). His father was a merchant, importing and selling a variety of goods, but apart from him Ibsen's paternal ancestors had, for as far back as we can trace them, over two centuries, been sea-captains. It came to be said of Henrik Ibsen that the older he grew the more he looked like a sea-captain himself; and the sea is a powerful and recurring element in his work, usually signifying the dangerous unknown which we fear and yet yearn for (as in *The Wild Duck, The Lady from the Sea* and *Little Eyolf*). When he was seven, his father lost all his money and the family had to move from its smart house in town to a humbler abode a few miles out. Bankruptcy was to become a spectre that would haunt Ibsen throughout his life and stalk grimly through one play after another.

Another such spectre stalked him early and permanently; illegitimacy. A boastful man in Skien named Tormud Knudsen (who, like so many boastful men, ended up as a Member of Parliament) had courted Ibsen's mother before her marriage, and claimed that he was Ibsen's father. The claim was almost certainly untrue, since Ibsen grew up to look very like his legal father and not at all like the much more handsome Knudsen; but children who despise their father as Ibsen did and hear rumours of their illegitimacy readily believe it, as Ibsen seems to have done. His plays were to be as full of illegitimate or supposedly illegitimate children as of bankrupts: Haakon Haakonson in *The Pretenders*, the Ugly Brat in *Peer Gynt*, Regina in *Ghosts*, Hedvig in *The Wild Duck*, Rebecca West in *Rosmersholm*.

At fifteen Ibsen left school and went to work at an apothecary's in the tiny port of Grimstad a further hundred miles down the coast, where he remained for six years. The work was arduous; apart from doing most of the work in the shop, since the apothecary was lazy and often drunk, he also had to run the post office and dole out the sweets. But he was one of those people who can manage on four hours of sleep, and he somehow found time to read for his matriculation, studying among other subjects Greek and Latin, and also to paint and write poems. His earliest ambition was to be a painter, and it was lucky that his father lost his money, for in those days there was no advanced school of painting in Norway, and he obviously could not go abroad. His son Sigurd later remarked that as a result the world gained a great writer at the expense of a bad painter; such of Ibsen's paintings as have survived are very pedestrian. He also wrote a good deal of poetry. Poetry, not prose, was his first love, and he later said that the former came more easily to him.

At the age of eighteen he, who so dreaded illegitimacy, fathered a son on one of the servant-girls at the apothecary's, ten years his senior. She went away to have the child, and it is doubtful whether Ibsen ever saw him, though he had to pay paternity costs from his almost non-existent earnings for fourteen years. At twenty-one, in his tiny bedroom, he wrote his first play: a verse tragedy, *Catiline*, about the kind of rebel that Ibsen himself already was and, in his way, was always to remain.

He passed his matriculation and entered Christiania University, still intending to become, if possible, a painter, otherwise a doctor; he had learned a lot about medicine at the apothecary's. He wrote a second play, another verse tragedy called *The Warrior's Barrow*, set in Viking times; and a friend who had come into a tiny inheritance nobly gave it all to pay for a private printing of *Catiline*, which predictably aroused so little interest that they finally sold what remained of the edition to a pedlar in exchange for enough to buy one decent supper for them both. It was mere chance that led him to enter the theatre as a profession.

Norway was ruled by Sweden, as Ireland by England, and culturally she was a province of Denmark; plays had to be written in

Danish, most of the best parts were taken by Danes, and such Norwegians as did appear had to cultivate a Danish accent. Indignant at this state of affairs, the people of Bergen, the second city in Norway, decided to start a National Theatre, and persuaded their most distinguished citizen, the composer and violinist Ole Bull, to lead it. He applied for a government grant to get it going; the government refused. Nowhere was this meanness more hotly debated than at the Students' Union in Christiania, and no one spoke out more vehemently against it than the young Ibsen. Bull heard of this, and of the fact that the young man had written a couple of plays, and offered Ibsen the job of general dogsbody (though he did not put it that way) at the new theatre, at a salary of five pounds a *month*, which even in those days was pretty marginal. He would have to direct plays, keep the accounts, design costumes, instruct the actors and, most importantly, write a new play each year. He did not know anything about any of these things, but nor did any other Norwegian. The fact that he had just failed his preliminary examination in Greek and mathematics no doubt helped Ibsen's decision; so, at the age of twenty-three, he left Christiania for Bergen.

Enterprisingly, the Bergen Theatre forthwith despatched him and their most promising young actor and actress to study theatre abroad for three months in Copenhagen and Dresden, and in Copenhagen Ibsen saw Shakespeare acted for the first time: *Hamlet, King Lear, Romeo and Juliet* and *As You Like it*. He also saw four comedies by Ludvig Holberg, the gifted eighteenth century Norwegian disciple of Molière; from him Ibsen learned the art of keeping the action of a play moving, a debt which he was frequently and gratefully to acknowledge. In Dresden he saw another production of *Hamlet* and, almost certainly, *A Midsummer Night's Dream*. Full of excitement and ambition he returned to Bergen and, in the six years that he was there, wrote flop after flop.

Some authors develop early; Dickens wrote *Pickwick* at the age of twenty-four. But Ibsen was a failure until he was thirty-six. Those early plays of his are never performed now even in Norway, except very occasionally as curiosities. There are several reasons for their lack of quality; indeed, considering the state of the drama in Europe then, it would have been surprising if they had been otherwise. The Bergen Theatre being a National Theatre, he was expected to write about Norway's glorious past, but unfortunately Norway had not had any glorious past for about five hundred years, which meant that he had to set his plays in either the Middle Ages or the Viking period, around 1000 A.D.; and there was little native literature to inspire him. Apart from Holberg's plays, there were only the mediaeval ballads and folk tales, and the ancient sagas, none of them a useful model for a dramatist. Moreover, he was a poor director, imaginative in his staging but timid in his dealings with actors. What is interesting to us about those early plays of his, the complexity of the characters, was precisely what most irritated the critics and audiences. Ibsen already knew that in a serious literary work no character is wholly good or evil, but that everyone is a mixture of the two; but this baffled his contemporaries, who liked to know who was good and who bad. (This attitude was to bedevil Ibsen throughout his career; we find critics laying the same complaint about *The Wild Duck* as late as 1884). At the same time, Ibsen's early plays were better than any other serious plays being written at that time outside Russia, where Ostrovsky and Turgenev had begun their careers, though their plays were unknown outside Russia. The only other contemporary plays that have survived into the modern repertory are the farces of Eugène Labiche, such as *An Italian Straw Hat*, which Ibsen admired and directed twice.

In 1857 he was offered the job of artistic director at a new National Theatre, in Christiania. He accepted eagerly; the salary was better, at any rate on paper, and he was glad to get away from the provincialism of Bergen. Alas, his six years in Christiania were to prove worse than his six in Bergen. The audiences, critics and actors of the capital were no more interested in the kind of thing Ibsen wanted to write and direct than the Bergensers had been. And the theatre seldom had the money to pay his full salary, so that he found himself even worse off financially than before. A year after his arrival in Christiania, he married the daughter of the Dean of Bergen, Suzannah Thoresen, a formidably emancipated young lady who was to prove a tower of strength to him throughout his life, and the following year their only child, Sigurd, was born. These were almost his only consolations. He had a small success with *The Vikings at Helgeland*, a Wagnerian kind of play; but a more characteristic work, *Love's Comedy*, about the incompatibility of love and marriage, was rejected by his own theatre, and he, as he later put it, was consequently 'excommunicated'. He had to eke out his living by writing hack poems to celebrate the opening of a new school, or the anniversary of a rifle club, and became an alcoholic. It was a common sight for the students of Christiania to see his squat bearded figure lying helpless in the gutter. Moreover, his frequent applications for a writer's pension were rejected, though these were generously handed out to other writers now long forgotten.

Then in 1864, when he was thirty-six, Ibsen's luck changed. He wrote his first great play, *The Pretenders*; he directed it himself (the last play he was ever to direct), and it was a success. And he received, at last, a pension of one hundred pounds for life – not much, but just enough for a man to live on parsimoniously. He made an immediate decision to turn his back on the two things that he hated most and that had most humiliated him: Norway and the theatre. Determined to write no more plays, he left for Rome. He was to spend the next twenty-seven years in self-imposed exile, and was to write most of his great plays there – in Italy, Dresden, Munich, Italy again and Munich again – before returning to spend the last fifteen years of his life in Norway at the age of sixty-three.

Italy exhilarated him, especially the great art galleries. Ibsen still had ambitions as a painter, and in those days, when photography was still in its infancy, and illustrations were engravings, a man had to see the originals. Michelangelo especially attracted him – unfashionably, for Michelangelo was regarded then as a gifted barbarian, inferior to Raphael. But in Michelangelo, Ibsen recognised a kindred spirit, a bleak and lonely artist like Milton, Wordsworth, Carlyle, Herman Melville and himself; and Michelangelo's unfinished statues, which Ibsen must surely have seen during his brief stay in Florence on his way to Rome, mighty figures straining to release themselves from the marble imprisoning them, foreshadow the chained creatures whom Ibsen was to create in words as Michelangelo had in stone.

Retiring to a village outside Rome, Ibsen began an epic poem in which he castigated many aspects of Norwegian society. But after completing fifty pages, as good as anything he had yet written, he encountered a block and could get no further. Then, going into Rome, he strolled into St Peter's and there, looking up at Michelangelo's roof in the Sistine Chapel, 'everything I wanted to say suddenly appeared to me in a strong and clear light'. Putting aside his unfinished poem he rewrote it as a play – but as a play to be read, not acted. So discredited was the drama among men of letters then that several, such as Musset and Turgenev, had adopted this form. Ibsen called his play *Brand*, and, since he was writing not for the horribly limited theatre of his experience but for a theatre which existed only in his imagination, he was able to create characters and relationships of a complexity which would utterly have baffled the actors and audiences of Norway, and to include such scenes as a storm at sea and an avalanche. He wrote it in rhymed verse, splendidly pointed and flexible. It was published, and was a huge success. For the first time in his life, he even made a little money, some of which he forthwith spent on his private passion, clothes.

Today, *Brand* excites us as a mighty tragedy of a great but misguided spirit, like Lear. It was not as such that it made its author's name in Scandinavia. What most delighted his contemporaries were the long passages of satire which today seem most dated and dispensable. To them it was a new *Candide*. It is a measure of the gulf between Ibsen's imagination and the theatre of his time that despite the play's success with the reading public, it was nineteen years before anyone tried to stage it (and then not in Norway).

Ibsen followed *Brand* with a similar kind of play, to be read, not acted. He made his new hero the exact opposite of Brand. Brand was a man who refused to compromise and by his misguided single-mindedness destroyed everyone and achieved nothing. Ibsen's new hero, Peer Gynt, was a trimmer whose life was one whole compromise and evasion, and who, like Brand, destroyed himself. *Peer Gynt* was a success, though a lesser one than *Brand*, but it too struck people as impossible to stage. It had to wait seven years for its premiere; Grieg did the music, as unsuitable an accompaniment as has ever been written for a play by a major composer; for over a century it caused directors, actors, and readers to regard that harsh tale, as harsh as *Brand*, as a jolly fairy story. Grieg, though a good friend of Ibsen's, then and always, disliked the play and Ibsen disliked the music. However much one may enjoy it for its own sake, one hopes never again to hear it in connection with any stage production.

Ibsen was now thirty-nine, and if he had died – if one of those tiles which he always feared might blow off a roof in a high wind and brain him had in fact done so – he would have been unknown outside Scandinavia and remembered there as a failed playwright and theatre director who had written two good verse satires in play form that could never be acted and would probably be forgotten once the targets of their satire had faded. Who, even Ibsen himself, could have foretold that he would hardly write another line of poetry and that he would, in prose, become the most influential playwright of his time or since?

He left Rome for Dresden (because there were good educational facilities for foreigners there and there were problems about his son's attending Catholic school in Italy). There, in the next six years, he wrote *The League of Youth*, a rangefinder for the 'modern' prose plays to come, and *Emperor and Galilean*. *The League of Youth* is a comedy, almost a farce, about the kind of left-winger that Ibsen, then as always a left-winger, most distrusted, a Peer Gynt of politics. *Emperor and Galilean* was an epic drama in the mould of *Brand* and *Peer Gynt* and likewise not intended for the stage, about the Roman Emperor Julian the Apostate who abandoned Christianity for paganism. When it appeared, Edmund Gosse, Ibsen's first pioneer in England, published a review in the *Spectator* regretting Ibsen's abandonment of verse, and Ibsen wrote him a letter explaining his change of medium. 'The illusion I wanted to create,' he declared, 'is that of reality. I wished to produce the impression on the reader that what he was reading was something that had really happened. . . . We are no longer living in the age of Shakespeare. . . . My new drama is no new tragedy in the ancient acceptation; what I desired to depict was human beings, and therefore I would not let them talk in "the language of the gods".'

Also in Dresden, Ibsen gathered his poems (excluding the poetic dramas) into a volume of about a hundred pages and published them, as though in farewell to the medium that had at last brought him fame. Then he moved to Munich and, over the next quarter of a century, composed the twelve great prose plays from which the whole of modern drama (not merely prose drama) stems.

The first four of these, *The Pillars of Society* (1877), *A Doll's House* (1879), *Ghosts* (1881) and *An Enemy of the People* (1882) are usually categorised as sociological dramas. It was a phrase Ibsen disliked; he protested that they dealt only secondarily with social problems and were primarily, like all his plays, first and foremost about individuals and relationships. Even *A Doll's House*, he was to assure the Norwegian Society for Women's Rights, was not about women's rights but human rights, the need for every being, be he man or be she woman, to find out who he or she really is and to become that person. He disliked people concentrating exclusively or overmuch on this aspect of his plays. And their survival today justifies his claim. We act and watch them not for the problems they debate but for their human drama.

Nevertheless, what excited his contemporaries and caused these plays to spread throughout the Western world and make the theatre something it had not been since Grecian times was the fact that they discussed, in dramatic form, the kind of topic about which people argued in newspapers and debating societies and on street corners. Euripides had done this, but no playwright since, or anyway not with the same force and effect. People emerged from Ibsen's plays compelled to rethink many basic concepts, some of which they had not before seriously questioned. Did the means justify the end in politics? Had a woman the right to leave her husband and children? Could incest, under certain circumstances, be justified (one of the themes of *Ghosts*, where Mrs Alving feels that Oswald's only hope of salvation may be a liaison with his half-sister Regina)? No one ever came out of a Shakespeare play with such huge question-marks in his head. Other writers had of course raised these or similar questions in novels, but Ibsen knew that a man may more easily be moved in a crowd than alone in his home, and it was this that made him a more influential moulder of opinion and general shaker-up than even Dickens or Zola. No wonder the young Bernard Shaw, who discovered Ibsen from William Archer, who happened to occupy the next desk in the British Museum Reading Room, realised, as Archer translated such plays as *A Doll's House* to him off the cuff, that this, not the novel or the pamphlet, was the medium through which a thinker might most effectively spread his gospel.

The Pillars of Society spread Ibsen's fame to Germany; in Berlin alone it was staged at five separate theatres within a fortnight. (And only one of these paid him anything; the others were able to pirate his work with immunity because Norway and Denmark had not signed the Berne Copyright Convention – the reason being that most of their school textbooks in arithmetic and the like were foreign and they did not want to have to start paying for the rights to use them; Ibsen complained that he was thus unwillingly subsidising most of the school textbooks of Norway). *A Doll's House* spread his fame throughout the Western world – not at once, but over the next decade. *Ghosts*, though at first rejected by the bookshops and theatres, established itself once it had been staged in Sweden two years after publication, and *An Enemy of the People* was a popular success.

Of the main character in that play, Ibsen wrote: 'In ten years the majority may have reached the point where Dr. Stockmann stood when the people held their meeting. But during those ten years the doctor has not stood stationary; he is still at least ten years ahead of the others. . . . I myself feel a similarly unrelenting compulsion to keep pressing forward.' It was characteristic of Ibsen, something of a trimmer, a Peer Gynt, a Pontius Pilate in his private life, but a brave man in the more lasting medium of print, that he did not rest upon his laurels nor try to repeat his triumphs. Just as he had abandoned the successful form of *Brand* and *Peer Gynt* for that of *A Doll's House*, so now he was to abandon topical debate for plays that dealt more or less exclusively with human relationships.

The Wild Duck (1884) seemed to contradict one of the principal dogmas that Ibsen had been preaching: the importance of ideals and the sin of compromise. Gregers Werle in that play enters a family that, like most families, lives on a variety of illusions and, by stripping them of these illusions, destroys them. The critics were much confused by this apparent self-contradiction on Ibsen's part, though in fact the message of *The Wild Duck* is not greatly different from that of *Brand*. And they complained that apart from Hedvig there was really no likeable character in the play, so that they did not know with which of the others they ought to sympathise. It was not as well received as the 'sociological' plays (apart of course from *Ghosts*) had been.

Rosmersholm, which followed in 1886, was even worse received, both on publication and in performance. In this play and its successor, *The Lady from the Sea*, Ibsen was investigating those dark forces that control our lives and impel our actions, exploring, as Strindberg was then (*Miss Julie* appeared in the same year as *The Lady from the Sea*), that same forest that the young Sigmund Freud was exploring, and arriving by the parallel path of intuition at the same goal which Freud was to reach by analysis. (Ibsen was Freud's favourite playwright, and *Rosmersholm*, on which Freud wrote a penetrating essay, particularly fascinated him.)

The Lady from the Sea, published when Ibsen was sixty, struck contemporary critics by the mellowness of its ending. It was the nearest thing to an optimistic play that he had written. But its successor, *Hedda Gabler* (1890), was black indeed, as were the four plays that followed.

The previous year, while holidaying in Gossensass in the Tyrol, he had met an eighteen-year-old Viennese girl named Emilie Bardach. She fell in love with him, and he with her; she wanted to go away with him, and he seems to have agreed to this. But when he returned to Munich with Suzannah (to make the necessary arrangements, as Emilie supposed) Ibsen chickened out of the plan. One can guess at the reasons: guilt at leaving Suzannah, who had been so much his driving force and comfort; an old man's doubt whether he could satisfy, or keep satisfied, a girl forty-three years his junior; fear of scandal. He wrote warmly to Emilie for four months, then broke off the correspondence. The incident had a profound effect on him. For years he had resigned himself to believing that romantic love was not for him. Now, at sixty, he found that, as Mr Graham Greene has remarked, fame is a powerful aphrodisiac. Other young girls, always artists, writers and the like, were to become infatuated with him, and he with them, though he almost certainly never slept with any of them. In sexual matters he seems to have been deeply inhibited; his doctor in his last years, Edvard Bull, told his son Francis, who told me, that Ibsen was preternaturally shy about exposing his sexual organ during medical examination, which struck Dr Bull as surprising from the author of *Ghosts*. And the discovery that what he must have longed for, and had assumed was not for him, was there for the taking and that he could not take it, must surely be responsible, mainly if not wholly, for the extreme pessimism of those five final plays.

Hedda Gabler might be subtitled: Portrait of the Dramatist as a Young Woman. Hedda has many of Ibsen's personal traits: the longing for sex and fear of it, the social snobbery, the dread of scandal. On publication and in performance, it was the worst received of all his mature plays, partly because of the alarming character of the protagonist, partly because in it Ibsen was reducing explanation to a minimum; it contains no long speeches in which the characters explain each other or themselves. Ibsen's enemies in Norway, of whom there were many, were quick to suggest that his powers were failing. Unfortunately for them, international interest in his plays was now enormous, and his compatriots found that, for the first time, a Norwegian author had become a world celebrity. People in many countries, including Thomas Mann and James Joyce, learned Norwegian solely to be able to read Ibsen in the original.

The year after writing *Hedda Gabler*, Ibsen, now sixty-three, returned to Norway, and spent the remaining fifteen years of his life there. Of the four final plays which he wrote there, three – *The Master Builder*, *John Gabriel Borkman* and *When We Dead Awaken* – deal with old men who have achieved fame in their chosen professions at the expense of leaving their emotional life a blank page, and who are suddenly offered what they have shunned and long for. Each of these plays likewise portrays a marriage, painfully identifiable as Ibsen's own, in which love, at any rate of the romantic kind, has long died. The fourth of these plays, *Little Eyolf*, is a work apart; it, too, deals with a dead marriage, but between younger people. The most sexually explosive of his plays, it is technically perhaps his most astonishing, in the subtlety of its tangled relationships and the almost complete absence of outward action in the last two tremendous acts.

After completing *When We Dead Awaken*, or perhaps while still working on it, Ibsen had the first of several strokes which were shortly to incapacitate him, and he spent the last five years of his life virtually paralysed and unable to write. He died in 1906 at the age of seventy-eight.

When *When We Dead Awaken* appeared, it greatly excited an eighteen-year-old Dublin student who begged the editor of the *Fortnightly Review* to be allowed to review it. His request was granted, and the result, a penetrating panegyric, caught Ibsen's notice in Norway. He wrote to his Scottish translator, William Archer (the letter is in the British Museum): 'I have read, or rather, spelt out, a review by Mr. James Joyce in *Fortnightly Review* which is very benevolent and for which I should greatly like to thank the author, if only I had sufficient knowledge of the language.' Archer conveyed the message to Joyce, who, a year later, on the occasion of Ibsen's seventy-third birthday, wrote Ibsen a long fan-letter in his newly-acquired Norwegian. That letter has not survived, but luckily Joyce's command of Norwegian was not sufficient for him to write it off the cuff; he first penned a draft in English. That has survived (it can be read in Richard Ellmann's biography of Joyce) and remains the most eloquent and moving of tributes to the old century from the new.

3 Ibsen on the English Stage: '*The Proof of the Pudding is in the Eating*'

INGA-STINA EWBANK

The vast and vague title of this paper has been staring me in the face ever since I accepted the invitation to speak to the Vancouver Conference on Ibsen. Whatever it might suggest, I do not intend to attempt the task, so ably performed by many others, of tracing the fortunes of Ibsen on the English stage, nor the possibly more intriguing task of defining Ibsen's function as, in Henry James's words, 'a sort of register of the critical atmosphere, a barometer of the intellectual weather'.[1] I simply want to speak, from a limited experience as a translator, of some problems involved in putting Ibsen texts on the contemporary English stage, and of the light thrown by those problems on Ibsen's dramatic and verbal structures. My subtitle is therefore the working title of a general rather than specific inquiry into whether, how, and why the Ibsenite pudding is eaten by English audiences.

I must, however, confess that I find an ironic aptness in the maxim itself: the proof of the pudding is in the eating. As a view of value and a definition of truth, it is just the kind of quintessentially 'English' statement which we would expect the Ibsen of *Brand* – and indeed of most of the other twenty-four plays – to deplore. It is surely no coincidence that this axiom has no equivalent in the Scandinavian languages, nor that it is (as far as I can ascertain) quite untranslatable into any of the Germanic languages. In a lecture recently, on 'Brecht and English Literature', John Willett recounted a German effort at translation which, translated literally back into English, goes: 'the proof of the pudding lies in the fact that you eat it' – thus not only transforming a pragmatic proverb into a metaphysical statement but also freezing into a static and absolute

27

proof of existence that which the English version implies to be a dynamic process during which a mixture of impulses may pass from the pudding to the eater. In the original, it embodies English empiricism and a tradition of compromise which to outsiders, particularly North Europeans, has always tended to seem morally lax, limp, flaccid – all those adjectives which could be used to translate Ibsen's word *slapp*. This is the word with which Brand loves to whiplash his fellow humans, including the doctor who brings him the news of his mother's death:

> Human! Ja, dette slappe ord
> er feltrop for den hele jord!

> Humane! That flaccid word
> Is now the motto for the whole wide world![2]

With this word, too, Ibsen in his last play holds doom-session over himself, as he makes Irene attack Rubek for being a '*dikter*', evading personal responsibility by hiding behind his art. In a virtually untranslatable matching of sound to scorn she identifies his ability to survive as a matter of being '*slapp og sløv og full av syndsforlatelse for all ditt livs gjerninger og for alle dine tanker*' ('lax and soft and full of self-forgiveness for all you have done in your life, and for all you have thought').[3] And, though the word itself does not surface, the rejection of all that is *slapp* informs the letter which Ibsen wrote to his mother-in-law soon after finishing *Brand*, explaining that he did not want to return to Norway because his own son 'shall never, if I can help it, belong to a people whose aim is to become Englishmen rather than human beings'.[4]

Clearly it would be wrong to make too much of an Anglophobia which, like Brand's fulminations against British industrialism and the race it produces, of 'hunch-backed souls and bodies',[5] is in any case ultimately an attack on his own country, and against which should be set the Anglophilia of his correspondence, later in life, with Gosse and Archer. All the same, Ibsen's refusal, in 1865, to allow full human status to *slapp* Englishmen points to what I think must be the root of his alienness in England (i.e. to feelings about him which go far deeper than any of the shifting attitudes to whatever version of Ibsenism happens to be current): his concern with total personal commitment. *Brand* may be his most explicit onslaught on 'the spirit of compromise'; but in one way or another all his plays, from *Catilina* to *When We Dead Awaken*, explore the central characters' vision of their own selves and test the strength of their 'calling'. With (I hope) every awareness of the dangers of generalising, and as a naturalised outsider too, I feel that the great tradition of English literature would favour a Dorothea Brooke's learning to appreciate 'an equivalent centre of self'[6] in others, over and against a Brand's pursuit of true selfhood at the expense of others. Students of English, to whom Ibsen has become, as James McFarlane has taught us to say, 'naturalised by syllabus', naturally put him in his 'period' of mid- and late-Victorian literature: alerted by an apparent similarity of theme, they soon find a world of difference between the single-mindedness of Arnold's Scholar Gipsy (who had *'one* aim, *one* business, *one* desire') and Ibsen's Brand. They may admire the formal perfection of Ibsen's plays over the 'fluid puddings' (Henry James) into which the main imaginative energies of English literature went in the period; but they will also point out that the best Victorian novels are large, loose and baggy in shape precisely because they are intent on bringing the reader to the realisation that 'to lace ourselves up on formulas [like "All or Nothing"] is to repress all the divine promptings and inspirations that spring from a life vivid and intense enough to have created a growing insight and sympathy . . . a wide fellow feeling with all that is human'.[7] The statements on the death certificates of Maggie Tulliver and Rebekka West may be identical; and Maggie's drowning, her arms round her brother, may be a melodramatic accident; but it celebrates a selfless impulse, not a ritual, self-authenticating suicide.

English tradition continues to feel uneasy about single-mindedness, and to find the total devotion to a calling somewhat embarrassing: at best, absurd and simplistic; at worst, pernicious. 'No man', Peter Stern remarks laconically in his recent book on Nietzsche, 'came closer to the full realisation of self-created "values" than A. Hitler'.[8] When the National Theatre production of *Brand* opened in the Oliver Theatre at the end of April 1978, its reception by the critics registered just that kind of unease: a puzzlement at and revulsion from Ibsen's dramatisation of the life and death of Brand in (as the *Observer* put it) 'highly symbolic circumstances'. The feeling that Ibsen's territory was alien dominated even the captions of the reviews. 'The Uphill Climb Leads to Stony Ground', complained the *Daily Mail*, and *The Times* found the climb both arduous and futile: 'Up the Icy Path: Ibsen

Unconquered'. Perhaps predictably, the *Daily Telegraph*'s critic saw
the play as something of a tract for the *slapp* times we live in, and
admired 'the stern idealist slamming wily politicians'; but he then
went on to lament that 'Ibsen has not found concrete situations to
express effectively his hero's immortal longings and internal
struggles', and that 'nor is it ever quite clear whether the play is
intended to exalt its uncompromising hero or condemn him for his
lack of Christian charity'. The most considered statement came
from *The Times*, where Irving Wardle found that the figure of Brand
was portrayed, in this production, with insufficient 'spiritual
turmoil' and 'mesmeric authority', and that therefore 'we are
left . . . at the mercy of everything that still repels people in Ibsen –
the naive symbolism, intellectual fog and maudlin sadism'.[9]

These criticisms may not be academically respectable – though
they certainly affected the box-office and hence the length of time
the play was kept in repertory – but I have quoted them precisely
because it is so easy to forget, in academic contexts and in gatherings
of the converted, like this Conference, how alien Ibsen can seem.
Nor is it simply a question of academic versus popular appeal. The
last twenty-five or thirty years have witnessed some avid eating of
the Ibsen pudding in the English theatre – notably the felicitous
results of the collaborations between Michael Meyer as translator
and Michael Elliott as director – but posterity will not be able to tell
this from published accounts of the stage in the period. Kenneth
Tynan's *View of the English Stage, 1944–63* (1975) mentions, apart
from *The Master Builder*, only *The Lady from the Sea* – significantly,
'the only Ibsen play that Chekhov might have written'; and when
Ruby Cohn writes of *Currents in Contemporary Drama* (1969), Ibsen is
not a 'current', nor does he even figure in the index. On paper,
Ibsen would seem to have little to offer the English theatre in the
seventies: Frederick Lumley, in *New Trends in Twentieth-Century
Drama* (4th rev. ed., 1972), finds that 'the theatre of Ibsen belongs to
another age', and that his plays 'seem no longer to express an age in
transition, where everything is uncertain and dominated by an
inquietude, and blind groping for a way of life in a civilisation where
crisis has become normality'.[10] Yet, when the National Theatre in
the early part of 1975 mounted both *John Gabriel Borkman* and
Pinter's *No Man's Land*, both directed by Peter Hall and starring
Ralph Richardson, then not only was Ibsen's play a popular success
but it clearly seemed to audiences to express, as much as Pinter's, all
those uncertainties, 'trendy' or not, which Mr Lumley would deny

him. All one can say is that those who eat and those who analyse the pudding appear to come away with different experiences: as if an Ibsen play stood back from and regarded as a static phenomenon (the 'All-Or-Nothing Epic' of the *Observer's Brand*, for example) is something crucially different from the play experienced, moment by theatrical moment, in a performance. That this is so, may have something to do with what we may call – if we forget about Shaw – the quintessence of Ibsenism; and it leads me to the two points I wish to make in this paper. Of course it is dangerous to generalise about Ibsen, who we all know has a Janus face and tends to turn, with a *tvertimot* ('on the contrary'), on any single conclusion we may think we have reached. But I take some comfort from the fact that my two points in themselves form a dialectic argument, one which hinges on a *tvertimot*.

Simply, then, I believe that there is in Ibsen's dramatic work, from an English point of view (i.e. from the point of view of anyone brought up in the English language and on English literature), a profound and ineluctable alienness: an otherness which we suppress, or 'naturalise', at the risk of losing his uniqueness and turning him into a Henry Gibson. But I also believe that there is an otherness which need not be alien: one which becomes so only if we fail honestly to try to see what he is doing with the form and language of drama, and why. This second point has much to do with the much-quoted and often misused[11] definition of his own art which Ibsen gave in his 1874 speech to the Christiania students, when he not only told them that '*at digte*' ('to be a writer') meant '*at se*' ('to see') but also stressed, as equally '*vaesentlig*' ('essential'), that aspect of the creative act which involves controlling and structuring the perceptions of a reader or an audience: '*at se saaledes, at det sete tilegnes af den modtagende, som Digteren saa det*' ('to see in such a way that what has been seen is experienced by the recipient as the writer saw it').[12] Attention to both points is necessary if we are not to end up on either the Scylla of enforced naturalisation or the Charybdis of unfair deportation. Moreover, both points issue from qualities in Ibsen which, ultimately, operate in interaction: an interaction which, to me, characterises the unique Ibsen – the one who forms a nation of *one* and writes no language but his own.

First, the ineluctable otherness. I take this to be lodged in the vertical structure of the dramatic world he creates, and the demands of strenuousness and intensity he thereby makes both of actors and audience. In Chekhov, people long to be other than they are, or elsewhere (and often, as in *Three Sisters*, the two longings are the same). In Ibsen, they strive to be themselves, which means striving to fulfil their highest possibilities. Chekhov's characters try to avoid the shattering experience of self-confrontation; Ibsen's spend much of their time trying to '*grunne til bunns*' (literally: 'think through to the bottom') who they are, and why they are as they are. Their forward movement in dramatic time cries out to be seen, 'spatially', as a vertical thrust: upwards, to the peaks to which they aspire, and downwards, into the abysses to whose *bunn* they wish to penetrate. I doubt if any English writer, short of Milton in the huge vertical poem of *Paradise Lost*, so insistently arranges his material on a scale of 'down' and 'up'. In Ibsen, of course, the Christian landscape of Hell-Earth-Heaven has been replaced by the inner landscape of human minds. It goes, I hope, without saying that I am not trying to define the metaphysical structure of Ibsen's beliefs, or his private mythology, his desires and anxieties. I am merely attempting to define the main, stress-bearing structure of his dramatic world. Nevertheless, it is obvious that at its two extremes the vertical thrust tends to be fatal to the dramatic protagonists: with a very few exceptions they do not, despite the 'desperate triumph' of Hilde Wangel's last speech, get 'right to the top' before they die in the attempt; and the abyss into which they stare claims its victims, too – Hedda Gabler (I think) and Rosmer and Rebekka (certainly). At either extreme, too, there may be mysterious forces at work, mythologies which fit where they touch. Ibsen repeatedly makes use of a hovering analogy with Christ's temptation on a high mountain, for example;[13] and in the depths of the mountain mines, or the bank vaults, John Gabriel Borkman communes with spirits in a dimension which we surely feel to be more than psycho-pathological. At various stages in his career the vertical trajectory has no doubt been influenced by external idealogies: the strenuousness of Brand's commitment owes a great deal to Kierkegaard, the ruthlessness of Borkman's to Nietzsche. But the wholeness and consistency of this as a dramatic dynamism is all Ibsen's own. From the first words of Catiline, in his first play –

> *Jeg må! Jeg må; så byder meg en stemme*
> *i sjelens dyp, – og jeg vil følge den.*
> *Kraft eier jeg, og mot til noe bedre,*
> *til noe høyere, enn dette liv.*

(1, 3)

I must! I must! thus bids me a voice
In the depths of my soul – and I will follow it.
Strength have I, and courage for something better,
For something higher, than this life.

to the last lines of Irene, in his last –

*Ja, gjennem alle tåkene. Og så helt opp til tårnets
tinde, som lyser i soloppgangen.*

(III, 551)

Yes, through all the mist. And then right up to the
very top of the tower, lit by the rising sun

the vertical urge dominates his drama. It is as natural for Catiline to amplify 'something better' into 'something *higher*' as it is for John Gabriel Borkman to assume that his own 'other motives' must be '*higher* motives' (III, 469); and Irene is, in that last moment before the avalanche tumbles her and Rubek down to their death, an epitome of all the Ibsen heroes and heroines who have striven to reach 'right up to the top'. In this context, the wording of Ibsen's famous speech to the Christiania students, as he describes what he has written, is far more than a rhetorical cliché:

Jeg har digtet paa det, der saa at sige har staaet høiere end mit daglige jeg . . .
Men jeg har ogsaa digtet paa det modsatte, paa det, der for den inadvendte Betragtning kommer tilsynes som Slagger og Bundfald af ens eget Vaesen.[14]

I have written of that which, so to speak, has stood higher than my everyday self . . .
But I have also written of the opposite, of that which, as we look into ourselves, appears like the dregs and sediments of our own being.

As we have so little non-dramatic writing from Ibsen's pen, it is particularly interesting to note that, in this dramatic monologue about his art, the 'action' is structured in the same up-down pattern as in his plays.

It is of the very nature of this pattern that it is often difficult to say when Ibsen is being abstract and when concrete, to tell whether his

characters are speaking literally or metaphorically. Are the heights
and the depths in the mind or in the mountains and seas of Norway?
More often than not the answer is of course 'both': the physical
geography which embodies (rather than merely accompanying) the
spiritual action in *Brand*, on the one hand, and *When We Dead
Awaken*, on the other, is never far from the more domesticated
settings of the intervening plays. Nor is it just that it can sometimes
be seen from the windows of parlours or garden-rooms – though the
sudden view of the sunrise on the unattainable, indifferent peaks at
the end of *Ghosts* makes for one of the most devastating moments in
Ibsen's work – but it informs the dialogue throughout with a lively,
tangible sense of place and movement. The 'storm' which 'comes
drifting' over Gunhild Borkman and 'engulfs' her and her belief in
Erhart's 'high' mission[15] is no less real than the storm in the second
act of *Brand*; the mystery of '*havsens bunn*' ('the bottom of the sea') in
The Wild Duck is felt no more acutely than that of '*bunnen*' ('the
depths') of Rebekka West's mind (III, 150). It is perhaps in the last
plays, from *The Master Builder* onwards, that outer and inner
landscapes most completely interpenetrate, with a self-evidence
which makes Borkman's final walk 'out into the storm of life' and up
the cold mountain-side as 'realistic' as the preceding indoor scenes.
But the sense of an actual vertical landscape is never absent from the
'contemporary' plays; it spills over not only into metaphors, explicit
or submerged, but also into the ordinary verbs and adverbs of the
dialogue. Characters think and feel and act in terms of '*opp*' ('up')
and '*ned*' ('down'), and plays as different as *Rosmersholm* and *Little
Eyolf* (not to mention the not-so-contemporary *Emperor and Galilean*)
could be seen as having their structures charted by those two
prepositions, used by themselves or as verb prefixes.[16] Coherences
like these make nonsense of the view of Ibsen's plays as prosaic
structures decorated with 'inert' symbols[17] – a term I have deliberately eschewed so far – and point to an extraordinary imaginative wholeness of conception before which questions of what is
prosaic and what symbolic fade in importance. When Karsten
Bernick untranslatably introduces his grand confession by inviting
his fellow citizens to '*kjenne meg til bunns*' ('know me as I really am'),
neither they nor he are aware of the ironic reminder of that literal
'*bunn*' to which he had so recently consigned the 'Indian Girl' and
all who sailed in her. But we are, and as he proceeds *not* to confess
this unspeakable sin, we become aware of the abyss yawning under
the apparently happy ending of the play.[18] *Pillars of the Community*

has one of the most prosaic, and certainly the socially densest, textures of all Ibsen's plays; yet even here a vertical shaft is opened, into depths which Bernick himself hints at as 'horrifying'.[19]

It is also of the nature of this pattern that it asks of the actors who have to embody it an intense inwardness combined with a pellucid matter-of-factness. If the intensity is lacking, the structure easily falls apart into absurdity: I, for one, have sat through a recent West End production of *Rosmersholm* which felt like 'Much Ado about the Mill-Race'. If the matter-of-factness is lacking – if the actors attempt to do the interpreting for us, signal with unspoken 'as ifs' those metaphors which ought to be utterly self-evident descriptions of the geography of their minds, etc. – then we get the heavy, portentous Ibsen. *Rosmersholm* becomes a play about the significance of white horses. Actors and directors do not have the help provided by analytical soliloquies, as in Shakespeare, nor the sustaining network of explicit motivations, as in English realistic drama of the early twentieth century. (In that respect, the demands made by Ibsen – that we listen to his silences and apprehend his characters' words as just the tips of icebergs – are more akin to those made by recent dramatists, like Pinter.) What they do have, by way of plot, is a series of events which seem to have been chosen in order to place the characters at '*veiens skille*' ('cross-roads' as in *Brand*): events which, in terms of ordinary plot logic, are often blatantly coincidental,[20] but which, in terms of a play's vertical structure, serve to thrust the characters upwards or downwards. It is a strenuous world these characters inhabit; its dynamism lies not in coincidences, not in what 'happens to' people[21], but in what they choose to do. And they choose as they do because, as Borkman puts it:

> . . . *jeg måtte det fordi jeg var meg selv, – fordi jeg var John Gabriel Borkman, – og ikke noen annen.*
>
> (III, 479)

> . . . I had to because I was me . . . because I was John Gabriel Borkman . . . and not somebody else.

Dramatically, they should affect us not so much by the kind of choice they make as by the intensity with which they commit themselves to their chosen way – '*den ubetvingelige kallelse inneni meg*' ('an irresistible calling inside me'), as Borkman has it in the same passage. His calling drew him downward, towards '*de bundne millioner*' ('millions imprisoned') which '*lå der* . . . *dypt i fjellene*' ('lay deep in the mountains'); but where he typifies all the Ibsen protagonists is in the heavy, insistent rhythm and in the language – unremarkable in diction but patterned by repetitions into obsessiveness – through which he expresses himself. No Shakespeare hero defines himself in this self-enclosed way; but Ibsen's do, at least from the moment Brand realises that the field of action to which he is called is the microcosmic world of the individual soul:

> *Innad; innad! Det er ordet!*
> *Dit går veien. Der er sporet.*
> *Eget hjerte, –* det *er kloden.*

(I, 454)

> Inward; inward! That is the word!
> There goes the way. There is the path.
> One's own heart, – *that* is the world.

Apart from the inevitable metrical differences, the patterns in which Brand and Borkman hammer away at their respective visions are much the same. And the same pattern – an ineluctable inward/downward movement – can be found over and over again, not just locally but dominating whole play structures, as we are forced, via external facts, to conscious motivations, to those depths where motivations and explanations dissolve into mysteries. '*Det grunner vi aldri ut til bunns*' (freely translated: 'We shall never plumb that question to its depths'), says Rosmer in reply to Rebekka's question as to whether he is following her, or she him, into the mill-race (III, 158). *Rosmersholm* is altogether the most obvious example of this pattern, its plot simply a series of visitations which gradually force the protagonists (and us) down to deeper and deeper levels of exploration (of what happened in the past, and why), until the suicidal plunge becomes, in the self-created logic of the structure, the self-evident final thrust. The movement is at one and the same time into the individual minds and into the universal question of the meaning of it all. At the end of *Emperor and Galilean*, Macrina, leaning over the dead body of Julian the Apostate, leaves in suspension the question of whether he was 'a sacrificial victim of Necessity' or 'a glorious, broken tool of the Lord' (II, 318–9). Her simple phrase, '*la oss ikke tenke denne avgrunn til bunns*' ('let us not think to the bottom of this abyss') is almost identical with Rosmer's; in both we are directed, through a final hint at the spiritual geography of the play, to an unthinkable and inexpressible mystery at the heart of the individual *and* the universe. We see the two held together in Ibsen's poem 'Bergmannen' ('The Mountain Miner'), just as they are in the imagination of John Gabriel Borkman. The mountain miner, having once thought to find in the depths of the mountain *'livets endeløse gåde'* ('the limitless riddle of life'), persists despite the hopelessness of the quest:

> *Hammerslag på hammerslag*
> *inntil livets siste dag.*
> *Ingen morgenstråle skinner;*
> *ingen håpets sol opprinner.*

(III, 563)[22]

> Hammer-blow by hammer-blow
> Until the last day of life.
> No ray of morning light;
> No sunrise of hope.

I have quoted this stanza because it so images, in its rhythm and language pattern, its own meaning; and furthermore because, in doing so, it also describes and defines the expression of the vertical drive in Ibsen's plays. Plot-steps become hammer-blows, and language becomes the verbal signs of the hammer-blows which the characters strike, until their sunless end. The imaginative wholeness is formidable – but actors are left with the problem of sustaining, through these signs, the drive and intensity belied by the surface of the plot and the language.

This drive, I would maintain, makes Ibsen peculiarly alien to the English imagination. The moral life in English literature tends to be lived horizontally. Peaks are reserved for epiphanies, like Wordsworth's on Mount Snowdon. Self-discoveries have traditionally been made on the Kent marshes, or the Midland flats, or in foggy London. Shakespeare's characters learn by being moved about horizontally: in and out of the 'green world' of the Comedies, through the sea (and *not* by plunging 'full fathom five') on to an island where they find their selves, 'When no man was his own' (*The Tempest*, v.i.213), and from where they will return to their initial positions. It cannot be just because there are no mountains in Warwickshire that Shakespeare does not take his tragic heroes up, or down into, mountains, literally or metaphorically.[23] (There were none in Skien, either.) When he puts them in a claustrophobic court, or an island fortress, or on a blasted heath, it is so that they may learn as much, or more, from their conflicts and contacts with other people as from voyages through their own interior landscape. Of course they have inner landscapes, with peaks as high and abysses as deep as anything in Ibsen, but the features of these landscapes do not provide the termini of their plays. Before his last scene Hamlet has abandoned self-searching with a 'readiness is all', and when he knows he is dying, his concerns become very much those of a Prince of Denmark. Othello dies 'upon a kiss', and Lear with his eyes fixed on Cordelia's lips, no thoughts but for her life. Their lives are essentially far more social than those of the protagonists in Ibsen's so-called 'social' plays. 'I am very sorry', says Hamlet to Horatio about his behaviour to Laertes on and in Ophelia's grave,

> For by the image of my cause I see
> The portraiture of his –
>
> (*Hamlet*, v.ii.75–6)

an exercise of the moral imagination which never occurs to a Brand or a Nora or a Rubek. In the vertical structures of Ibsen, suspended between the relentless light of the peaks and the utter darkness of the abyss, everything looks more categorical and absolute; there is little chance for fine shades and nuances to be seen. The horizontal worlds of Shakespeare, or George Eliot, or Henry James, know the extremes of light and darkness, too; but their main business is conducted in the more intriguing interplay of half-lights, where a bush may be a bear, a truth grey, and discriminations are less self-evident. To measure the distance between the two worlds, without implying a preference for either, we may compare what Maisie knew to what Hedvig knew. The uncompromising structure of the Ibsen world bears in on us particularly keenly in his endings. English endings, at least until fairly recent times, have tended to leave us with a sense that there are alternatives, and that life must go on. Hamlet's 'dying voice' establishes Fortinbras; and the obscure (and, we might think, frustrated) life of Dorothea Brooke becomes 'incalculably diffusive' of good. When Shakespeare's protagonists die, the plays take us outside their fates for a commentary, a sense that their sufferings have been vindicated, and often also a sense of a new beginning. Even in the desolation at the end of *King Lear*, 'we that are young' have some life to come. Not so, with a very few exceptions,[24] in Ibsen. There is no new beginning in the shadow-life left to Gunhild Borkman and Ella Rentheim. There is not even that kind of choric release from the 'speechless horror' of Mrs Alving: we leave the theatre with the image of her suspended, as it were, in an arrested scream. We may – and often do – feel that the hero or heroine, in dying, has achieved a personal triumph; but, with the exception of Hilde Wangel, there is usually no one in the play to present this view-point. Those left on stage strike us by the irrelevance, or worse, of their comments: 'People don't do things like that', or 'The dead wife took them'. Our experience of the play ends with the shock of the protagonist's death and with little or no help to absorb it. To explain this by the fact that Ibsen, unlike Shakespeare, wrote for a proscenium stage and had acquired, from his dramatic models, a taste for strong curtain lines, would be to obscure the function of his endings in his vertical structures. His plays have us, as it were, clinging to a sheer rock face, staring into the abyss below and stretching towards the peaks above. As they end, we are left, still clinging, with no plateau within reach on which we might have rested, purged and reassured. As we scramble to safety into the real world outside the play, to catch our buses or write our reviews, we realise that the curtain (if there was one) signalled not so much the end of the play's action as the beginning of its after-effects on us.

If there is any validity in my analogy, then Ibsen's language should bear part-responsibility for the vertical and rock-like effect of his plays; and my discussion has already suggested that this is so. At this point I merely want to look at some particularly 'alien' aspects of Ibsen's handling of dramatic language. Born into the Norwegian language, he never during the long years of exile wrote drama in any other. Whatever the reasons for his staunch monolingualism (which may be contrasted with the case of Strindberg, or Beckett), the plays suggest an interesting interplay between the potentials and limitations of Norwegian, on the one hand, and his own expressive needs, on the other. I am here rushing into an area where my only equipment is a certain Swedish–English bilingualism and an accompanying sense – subjective and impressionistic – of the varying possibilities of English as against the Scandinavian languages. English feels soft and pliable: the vast polyglot vocabulary urges one to pursue nuances of meaning; the ubiquitousness of submerged or faded metaphors, of puns and other forms of word-play, acts as a spur to the associative imagination; the malleable grammar encourages syntactic adventurousness. For the same reasons, the language can only too easily show signs of tiredness, of being used up: the simple threatens to turn into the banal, the familiar into cliché; repetitiveness can suggest a poverty of the imagination. In contrast, the Scandinavian languages feel hard and unyielding: a smaller and purer vocabulary, a correspondingly limited range of word-rhythms, a far more restricting grammar – all these make the medium more sonorous but (unless one is a Strindberg) less associative, and certainly less rich in nuances. On the other hand, they give a strength to simplicities, a durability to the homely, and emphasis to metaphors. English may be the more helpful medium for the intricacies and complexities of human relationships; the genius of the Scandinavian languages tends towards the larger-featured, more blatant rendering of extreme states of mind.

I have tried to be objective, but it will be obvious that in describing Ibsen's raw material I have also implicitly begun to define his relationship with it. If the language is 'hard', he is a hard master – not, like Shakespeare, one 'whose nature is subdu'd/To what it works in, like the dyer's hand' (Sonnet CXI), but one who hammers and chisels away at it, like a sculptor. Indeed, Ibsen's favourite analogies for his own art were the arts of the sculptor and the architect, whereas Shakespeare, in the sonnets at least, saw himself as a painter. I don't want to push this comparison beyond what is legitimate, but it seems to me helpful to think of Ibsen's way of working with material in terms of Adrian Stokes's theory of the carver in stone: 'one feels that not the figure, but the stone through the medium of the figure, has come to life'. Shakespeare's way, then, would be closer to Stokes's other category, 'the plastic conception', where 'the material with which, or from which, a figure has been made appears no more than so much suitable stuff for this creation'.[25] Shakespeare invents new words, achieves new effects by combining Germanic and Latinate elements of the existing vocabulary, plays with grammar to turn nouns into verbs (and *vice versa*) and makes his characters seem to be naturally thinking in images. Ibsen takes the words the language provides, hammers and hammers away at them – and we are all familiar with the key-words which punctuate the plays like 'hammer-blows' – until they seem to acquire an arcane quality of their own, over and above their semantic meaning; lays simple syntactic units end to end, like builder's bricks; beats words together into compounds which are not so much new words as a revaluation of old ones (*'lysræd'*, *'livsglæde'*); and so makes the thinking of his characters part of the entire architecture of each play. To illustrate these generalisations, two passages will have to suffice. First, Edgar after watching the sufferings of the mad Lear sees his own both reflected and minimised:

> But then the mind much sufferance doth o'erskip
> When grief hath mates, and bearing fellowship.
> How light and portable my pain seems now,
> When that which makes me bend makes the King bow –
> He childed as I father'd!
>
> (*King Lear*, III. vi. 106–110)

For the second, I can think of none better than one on which I have already written[26] – the closing lines of *John Gabriel Borkman*:

ELLA: *Det var nok snarere kulden som drepte ham.*

MRS B (ryster på hodet): *Kulden, sier du? Kulden, – den hadde drept ham for lenge siden.*

ELLA (nikker til henne): *Og skapt oss to om til skygger, ja.*

MRS B: *Du har rett i det.*

ELLA (med et smertelig smil): *En død og to skygger, –* det *har kulden virket.*

MRS B: *Ja, hjertekulden. – Og så kan vel vi to rekke hinannen hånden da, Ella.*

ELLA: *Jeg tenker vi kan det nu.*

MRS B: *Vi to tvillingsøstre – over* ham *vi begge har elsket.*

ELLA: *Vi to skygger – over den døde man.*

> (Fru Borkman, bak benken, og Ella Rentheim foran, rekker hinannen hendene.)

ELLA: It was the cold that killed him.

MRS B (*shakes her head*): The cold, you say? It killed him long ago.

ELLA (*nods to her*): And turned the two of us into shadows.

MRS B: So it did.

ELLA (*with a painful smile*): One dead man and two shadows . . . is what the cold has made of us.

MRS B: Yes . . . the cold heart. (*pause*). Now we two can join hands, Ella.

ELLA: I think we can . . . now.
MRS B: We two . . . twin sisters . . . over the man we both
loved.
ELLA: We two shadows . . . over the dead man.
(*Mrs Borkman, behind the bench, and Ella, in front of it, join
hands.*)

Both are choric passages, in the sense that they contemplate what
we have just witnessed on stage, draw a 'meaning' out of that event –
Lear's madness, Borkman's death – and mediate between the
protagonist's experience and ours. In both, the mediation comes
through speakers who record the impact upon themselves of what
they, and we, have seen. Here the similarity ends, for while the
whole burden of Edgar's lines is sympathy, in the most literal sense
of the word, Ella's and Mrs Borkman's are, equally literally, self-
centred: they speak of, indeed enact, a kind of numb acceptance of
the fatal collision of three selves. The choric quality of Edgar's
speech is underlined – in a play where the range of speech-modes is
particularly wide, and where the moments of crisis, especially at the
end, find their expression in inarticulateness – by the rhymes and by
the careful parallelisms of his statements. And yet the language itself
'appears no more than so much suitable stuff for this creation': by
the means which I have tried briefly to describe, Shakespeare mixes
and moulds its elements to subdue them to the service of Edgar's
pain – 'light and portable' – and his discovery of sympathy: 'He
childed as I father'd'. The contrast between this phrase and Ella's
last line – 'We two shadows . . . over the dead man' – holds the
essence of what I am trying to say about Ibsen's use of language.
Taken by itself, Ella's line could easily be accused of trying to
achieve a profound effect by banal, even clichéd, means; it is a
sitting target for those English critics who belabour Ibsen for the
absence from his language of Shakespearean inventiveness and
metaphorical 'volatility'.[27] The point is that Ibsen is not aiming for
any of those qualities, and that he is using the Norwegian language
as it can be used: so that, in Stokes's terms, 'one feels . . . the stone
through the medium of the figure has come to life'. 'The figure' in
this case is the pattern of the dialogue in which Ella and Gunhild
come together at last into a '*vi to*', the gap between them bridged,
visually and verbally, by '*den døde man*'. Ibsen is drawing on the
strength of the Norwegian language, not trying to pretend that the
'stone' is clay but hammering at the stone to bring out its 'life'. The

limited vocabulary, the regular stresses and the heavy rhythms – all these features have been rarified and used to form a pattern of repetitions and echoes which images the meeting of the two women, as '*skygger*', in a land beyond both hope and despair. The whole pattern – and indeed the whole play – bears down on that last line. I have already written on how Ella's and Gunhild's dialogue is informed by, and completes, the pattern of cold and deadness which begins to take shape the moment the whitehaired Ella enters the drawing-room where Gunhild is 'always cold', the snow driving outside, and Borkman's steps echoing from the floor above; and I have also written on the problems of translating such dialogue into English. Here it is enough to say that the language pattern is part of Ibsen's 'vertical' structure: it expresses three self-enclosed minds, each looking into its own 'abyss' and reaching towards its own 'heights'. The idiom is alien and stands to lose its dramatic power if we pretend that it is not.

It is ironically apt that the word upon which the twin sisters establish their reconciliation is '*hjertekulden*' ('the cold heart'). At key points in his plays Ibsen – to the despair of his translators – likes to hammer two words together into a compound which, as it were, will clinch a character's attitude to him or herself and to others. Norwegian shares with the other Germanic languages the facility for creating compounds, and Ibsen availed himself of it – more sparingly in his later plays but to the full in a play like *Brand*, where the hero's energy seems to need this particular form of expression. Coinages like '*margstjal*' ('stole, or drained, the marrow' – i.e. out of the people) and '*fjellklemt*' ('squeezed, or pinched, by the mountain'), which give concrete images of the village people's mental and physical plight, suggest that Ibsen could be as verbally inventive as Shakespeare when his subject warranted it.[28] When he wanted to be satirical, he could do a double-take and be inventively uninventive: the Dean's compounds are stock pulpit rhetoric, and the Mayor just cannot speak of 'poverty' as such; it has to be '*armodsdommen*' ('the curse of poverty'). But in Brand's visionary moments we see the will bending and beating the language itself into his service, and with a cryptic syntax and illogical linking of sentences go also strange and unexpected compounds. Agnes's vision is shaped by similar means, but to a different end. In Act IV, when she takes out and looks at the clothes which belonged to her dead baby, she has a speech almost entirely made up of descriptive compounds: '*Perlestukken,/ smertekrammet, tåredrukken,/. . ./. . . kroningskåpen/som han bar i*

offerdåpen' ('Pearl-embroidered, /Pain-squeezed, tear-drenched,/
. . ./ . . . the coronation robe/ Which he wore for his sacrificial
baptism'). As my attempt at a literal translation shows, this is
virtually untranslatable. But in the original it has an intensity which
goes some way towards defending the passage against Irving
Wardle's (and others') accusations of 'maudlin sadism'. Agnes
begins with a reference to what the garment actually looks like and
rises from there to a kind of religious intoxication which makes us
feel how it is that she can bear the inhuman sacrifice of the child as
long as she has this one little tangible link with what happened. To
struggle with the compounds in *Brand*, I have found, is to become
aware how carefully Ibsen hammers them together so as to guide
our responses to the speaker. At the beginning of Act IV there is a
scene between Brand and Agnes where what Brand has to say
sounds so nearly like religious cant that I cannot believe Ibsen did
not intend a contrast between Brand's auto-intoxication and the felt
concreteness of Agnes's emotions. Brand has lines like these to
describe what should be Agnes's mission in life:

> du skal rekke meg de fulle
> kjaerlighetens lesknings-skåler,
> slynge mildhets kappefold
> varmt innunder bringens skjold;

(I, 495)

> You shall hand me the full
> Refreshing cups of love,
> Wrap the cloak of tenderness
> Warmly under the armour of my chest;

and Agnes, by referring to what *is* – the child's body, in the
graveyard, '*på de kolde spåners pute*' ('on the pillow of cold wood-
shavings') – sets up a corrective. Her womanly and sympathetic
imagination is like Cordelia's lament that Lear had to hovel 'In
short and musty straw' (*King Lear*, IV. vii. 40); Brand's idealising
rhetoric is nothing so much as an anticipation of the mixture of
unctuousness and chauvinism in the speeches of a Rørlund. One
more twist, and his rhetoric would be clearly satirical in purpose.

By now it will be obvious that the pursuit of Ibsen's ineluctable
alienness has, willy-nilly, taken me well into the second part of my
argument: that there is in Ibsen an otherness which need not be

alien – if, that is, we look in an unbiassed fashion at what is actually there in his texts. Looking at his language, even at such detailed aspects of it as his use of compounds, has made it clear that the 'vertical' paradigm must be complemented by another, horizontal, one. The vertical structure is most fully apprehended in a 'spatial' approach; it gives an outline of the world as seen from the protagonist's point-of-view. As such, it is – as I hope I have shown – crucial in our experience of an Ibsen play. It explains why we could never simply condemn Brand for his lack of Christian charity, or see John Gabriel Borkman as a self-deluded embezzler, or find even Hedda Gabler trivial. But, at the same time as this view-point is impressed upon our imaginations, it is also corrected, or amended, or modified. An Ibsen play always knows more than its protagonist and keeps telling us so. The hero or heroine's vision and achievement are 'placed' by a number of means. Most directly, we are kept aware how they – from Catiline to Rubek – in pursuing their vertical trajectories slice through other lives, wrecking them. Even Nora, in this way, provokes ambivalent feelings at the end of her play; and even Hilde Wangel, in *The Master Builder*, finds it more difficult to be ruthless in the pursuit of her vision once she *knows* Aline Solness. Brand literally kills the ones he loves most, and Borkman has killed '*kjaerlighetslivet*' – the very ability to love and be loved – in Ella Rentheim. Ibsen knows as much about the fatal danger of self-centredness as any English nineteenth-century novelist – only, he lets us work it out for ourselves and makes us weigh it against the power of a self committed to a calling. Similarly, we have to do the work of assessing the sincerity, or the degree of delusion, in the protagonist's vision, even before the ending of the play calls it into question – and even then Ibsen is intent on leaving us in a state of suspended judgment. This principle is as true, though its application varies, for Brand as for Rubek, for Bernick as for Borkman. Ibsen does not let the language of his characters interpret *for* us, and it is important that his translators should not do so either: to take but a single example, they should not make readers and audiences believe that Borkman puts words of judgment in our mouth by referring to his own 'indomitable ambition' when he is in fact speaking of '*den ubetvingelige kallelse inneni meg*' ('an irresistible calling inside me').[29] Borkman's magnificent vision in his final scene must be felt as magnificent; what 'places' it is the dramatic context and the clash with Ella's vision of 'a warm and human heart', sold (in Borkman's own words) 'for the kingdom . . . the power . . . and the glory'. As here, and as in the scene between Brand and Agnes which I discussed, Ibsen relies a great deal on playing off against each other the idioms of two visions, not necessarily to come down on the side of either, but to make us appraise either by the contrast with the other. Nowhere is this more obvious, or more central to the play, than in *The Wild Duck*, where the limitations of Hedvig's vision bring out the very different limitations of Gregers Werle's, and where the simple, literal statements of Gina (malapropist as she may be) come very close to an explicit criticism of the pernicious unreality of Hjalmar's metaphors: '*Se på barnet, Ekdal!*' ('Look at the child, Ekdal!').

Examples offer themselves in numbers larger than this paper will hold; but it should be possible now to generalise by saying that Ibsen's 'horizontal' mode is a forward (in play-time) rather than upward-downward (in mental space) moving dynamism. It means that, as the play evolves, our relationship with it and with its characters may alter moment by moment. Ibsen controls our perception of the play – makes us 'see' it, in his own terminology, as he saw it – by keeping our judgments alert and open. Incidentally, this means that the range of emotional responses he provokes from us is wider than his English critics have tended to allow: the self-preoccupation of characters, dramatised as an inability to see or hear others, can be both comic and disastrous (and sometimes, in *Borkman* for example, both at the same time). Above all, it means that, in the theatre, the real figure in Ibsen's carpet is not a matter of static symbols, but of a pattern evolving all the time, as the carpet unrolls, up to the last word and gesture of the play. To come back to the closing moments of *Borkman*, their impact is the product of the whole play's evolution. The twin sisters stand together at the end of the play, as they did at the beginning; but now the inner cold has been translated into the outer landscape, and Borkman is a corpse, killed by 'a hand of ice', or 'a hand of iron ore'. *They* think they are talking of 'the cold heart' of Borkman only; *we* know that they are also talking about themselves. They know only the destructiveness of Borkman's vision; we know also its compulsive glory. We are, as it were, at the meeting-point of Ibsen's vertical and horizontal thrusts.

A much simpler way of saying what I have been trying to say in the last paragraph is that in Ibsen, too – whatever he might have felt about the sentiments of the axiom – the proof of the pudding is in the eating. One could also say that Ibsen's otherness is his peculiar dramatic and theatrical virtue. Its demands are great: the vertical structure demands of actors an ability to project intense inwardness; the horizontal structure demands sustained ensemble playing, with attention to the minutest details of the text; both together demand directors who trust Ibsen and audiences who are ready to be at once involved and detached – to stand, as Henry James has it, 'in an exceptionally agitated way'[30] before his plays. If this is a counsel of perfection, it is in the nature of Ibsenism to reach out for the unreachable; and at least those who pursue it could not be accused of aiming at being 'Englishmen, rather than human beings'.

NOTES

1. Henry James, 'On the Occasion of *Hedda Gabler*', *New Review* (June 1891); reprinted in Michael Egan (ed), *Ibsen: The Critical Heritage* (London, 1972), p. 234.

2. My quotations from the text of Ibsen's plays refer, for convenience, to *Henrik Ibsen: Samlede Verker*, ed. Didrik Arup Seip, 3 vols (Oslo, 1960): this quotation is from I, 484. The literal translations of Ibsen into English are my own; those from Borkman are from the printed text of the English version by myself and Peter Hall (London, 1975).

3. III, 537. It will be apparent that the Norwegian word *slapp* seems to condemn its own meaning by its sound.

4. Letter to Magdalene Thoresen, written from Rome on 3 December 1865. In *Henrik Ibsen: Samlede Verker (Hundreårsutgave)*, eds Francis Bull, Halvdan Koht and Didrik Arup Seip (Oslo, 1928–57), XVI (1940), 119.

5. I, 564 ('*puslingflokken . . ./ . . ./ går med puklet sjel og rygg*').

6. George Eliot, *Middlemarch* (Harmondsworth, 1970), p. 243.

7. George Eliot, *The Mill on the Floss* (London, 1961), p. 487.

8. J. P. Stern, *Nietzsche* (London, 1978), p. 79.

9. The following reviews have been quoted: *The Times* (Irving Wardle), *Guardian* (Michael Billington), *Daily Telegraph* (John Barber), and *Daily Mail* (Jack Tinker): all on 27 April 1978; *The Sunday Times* (Robert Cushman) on 30 April 1978.

10. For Kenneth Tynan, see p. 329 of his book; for Frederick Lumley, see p. 3.

11. See, e.g. Ronald Gray, *Ibsen – a Dissenting View: A Study of the Last Twelve Plays* (Cambridge, 1977), taken to task by James McFarlane in his review of Gray's book, *Themes in Drama*, I, ed. James Redmond (Cambridge, 1979).

12. *Samlede Verker (Hundreårsutgave)*, XV (1930), 393.

13. Noticed by many, including myself in *Contemporary Approaches to Ibsen*, I, ed. D. Haakonsen (Oslo, 1966).

14. *Samlede Verker (Hundreårsutgave)*, XV (1930), 394.

15. See III, 442.

16. One of the benefits of an Ibsen *Concordance* would be to be able to survey these significant Ibsen adverbs, prefixes and prepositions.

17. Cf. Michael Black, *Poetic Drama as Mirror of the Will* (London, 1977), ch. 10.

18. I have developed this point in a paper on *Pillars of the Community*, in *Themes in Drama*, 1; cf. pp. 93–4.

19. Cf. Bernick's '*I vil forferdes*', and my paper, above.

20. And therefore criticised, as by Gray, op. cit., for being 'fanciful', or failing to 'make sense'.

21. Without wishing to belabour particular translators, I have noticed that when an Ibsen character has '*opplevt*' ('experienced') something, translators, opting for the idiomatic phrase but obscuring the active and strenuous nature of the Ibsen world, render this as something having 'happened to' them.

22. Ibsen's first version of these lines (1850) is far less powerful: '*Saadan gaar det Slag i Slag/ Til han segner traet og svag/* . . .' Ibsen revised these two lines to their present reading in 1863.

23. The non-existent cliff on which Gloucester is perched for a fall (*King Lear*, IV.vi), to be cured of his despair, rather proves than disproves my point.

24. *Little Eyolf* might seem to be an exception, but I agree with James McFarlane about the 'intellectual and emotional dishonesty' of Allmers and the dubious ending of this play. See the Introduction to *The Oxford Ibsen*, VIII (Oxford, 1977).

25. Adrian Stokes, *The Quattro Cento*, in vol. I of *The Critical Writings of Adrian Stokes*, ed. Lawrence Gowing (London, 1978); and the article, 'Adrian Stokes, Critic, Painter, Poet', by Richard Wollheim, *Times Literary Supplement*, 17 February 1978.

26. In *The Yearbook of English Studies*, IX ('Theatrical Literature': Special Number), 1979, pp. 102–115.

27. Cf. Black, op. cit.

28. For '*fjellklemt*', cf. Shakespeare's 'sea-change'.

29. Cf. the otherwise excellent McFarlane translation, in *The Oxford Ibsen*, VIII, p. 207.

30. Henry James, 'On the Occasion of Hedda Gabler', in Egan, op. cit., p. 235.

4 Ibsen and the Scandinavian Theatre

LISE-LONE MARKER AND FREDERICK J. MARKER

A comprehensive stage history of Henrik Ibsen's plays is long overdue. When, as we must all hope it will, such a project finally does become a reality, a central place within it will be reserved for the history of Ibsen performances in the Scandinavian theatre–from the context of which he emerged as a dramatist and to which his plays have never ceased to bear a unique and seminal relationship. From the outset of his career, as a stage director in Bergen and subsequently in Christiania (now Oslo), Ibsen developed a keen sense of the practicalities and performance conditions of the living theatre that never left him. These early experiences as a director should not be neglected, for they sharpened his extraordinary sensitivity to the poetry of environment in the theatre. In staging the first productions of his own early saga dramas, he taught himself to write a carefully visualised, highly charged physical *mise-en scène* into his plays, aimed at concretising the psychological states and spiritual conditions of his characters and designed to create a specific mood that would enhance and strengthen the spiritual action. Costumes, settings, props and lighting effects remained, from the beginning of his career to its end, the syntax of his dramatic poetry.

Henry James once called Ibsen 'a sort of register of the critical atmosphere, a barometer of the intellectual weather', and in just this sense the lively stage history of his plays, in Scandinavia and elsewhere, comprises a vivid chronicle in miniature of the changing theatrical styles and audience tastes of the past century. Approaching the subject from a somewhat different angle, we recognise that the plays have also continued to represent, particularly to directors and designers in Scandinavia, a stimulating and sometimes daunting but always inescapable challenge. From the pioneering naturalistic productions of William Bloch and his contemporaries in the eighties, through such twentieth century stylisations as Gordon Craig's remarkable rendering of *The Pretenders* in Copenhagen, and down to Ingmar Bergman's imaginative contemporary paraphrases in our own time, the inspiration of the plays has animated a multi-directional quest for theatrical forms and images which could accommodate and amplify Ibsen's vision on the stage. It is to a few selected examples of this chronicle of changing approaches and this quest for renewed theatrical expressiveness that this paper proposes to address itself.[1]

I

As might perhaps be expected, some of Ibsen's earlier and less familiar plays have enjoyed an especially full and interesting stage life in Scandinavia. Among them, *The Pretenders*, the first of his dramas to gain a permanent place in the repertory of the Scandinavian theatre, boasts a vigorous and fascinating production history that would, in itself, provide an eloquent chronicle of changing theatrical styles and tastes. This expansive, five-act historical drama, the last of Ibsen's plays to draw upon the colourful pageantry of Norwegian history and saga for its subject matter, dramatises the irresistible power of a great calling and the paralysing effects of self-doubt. Haakon, the unswerving believer in his own heroic destiny and in his ability to effectuate his great kingly thought, contends with the vacillating and reflective Skule for Norway's throne, while the violent strife between them is deliberately fostered by the diabolical Bishop Nikolas, the power-hungry impotent whose avowed purpose in life is to set in motion a *perpetuum mobile* of discord and distrust in the world. The first production of this play, which was the last that Ibsen himself ever directed, was given at Christiania Theatre – where he functioned as artistic consultant at this time – early in 1864, and it succeeded in holding the stage for eight performances during that winter. P. F. Wergmann, who has been called by Roderick Rudler the first national scene painter in Norway, was called upon to design new scenery for this production, and even the services of a local antiquarian were enlisted in order to provide the proper thirteenth-century Norwegian flavour. The task of the play's first designer and director was thus not only to articulate the dramatic and atmospheric values of Ibsen's multiple, boldly contrasted stage pictures, but also to lend them historical 'appropriateness' and 'authenticity'. Wergmann's impressive designs (though they did not in fact win the unconditional approval of the Christiania production's reviewers) epitomise a general style of robust pictorial solidity that was to remain intrinsic to the play's romantic stage tradition.

During the decades that followed this first production of what has been called, in the *Oxford Ibsen*, the playwright's 'first real and incontrovertible masterpiece', the tradition of pictorial illusionism and historical exactitude continued to influence the many major revivals of the work that occurred both within and outside Scandinavia – by Johanne Luise Heiberg at the Danish Royal Theatre in 1871, by the Duke of Saxe-Meiningen in Berlin in 1876, by Fritz Ahlgrensson in Stockholm in 1879, and by Max Reinhardt at his Neues Theater in 1904, to single out only four of the more important ones. Thus, as Johannes and Adam Poulsen prepared to celebrate the twenty-fifth anniversary of their acting débuts in 1926, it was only natural that this solid and continuous performance tradition should attract the sons of Emil Poulsen (whose 'emotional realism' in the role of Bishop Nikolas had created a sensation in Fru Heiberg's famous production) to this play as the perfect vehicle for their jubilee. A crisis of some sort was inevitable, however, when the staunchly anti-traditional Edward Gordon Craig was called to Copenhagen to design and assist in directing the production at the Danish Royal Theatre. 'I have never been concerned in any attempt to show the spectators an exact view of some historical period of architecture', Craig later declared in the sumptuous portfolio of designs which he published to commemorate this production. 'I always feel that the great plays have an order of architecture of their own, an architecture which is more or less theatrical, unreal as the play.'[2] The kind of carefully detailed stage directions which characterise Ibsen's text were, as we know, never regarded with much tolerance by Craig: 'If you meddle with the tools of a trade,' he writes elsewhere, 'it is best to master them – and for a dramatic writer to add stage directions to his written play, and to omit to show how these directions are to be carried out, is to tinker. In the Greek and Elizabethan drama, you will find no stage directions.'[3] In the light of such Craigish pronouncements as these, it is probably self-evident to add that his non-representational approach to *The Pretenders* demonstrated an uncompromising repudiation of the accepted pictorialism of earlier productions. He eliminated the principle of successive décors entirely, in favour of a simplified architectural device – a permanent structure of platforms that could be localised, in a symbolic manner, by means of projections, occasional hangings, the deployment of non-representational set-pieces and small panels, and the selective use of central objects expressive of a particular scene's essential idea.

It would be a mistake to assume, meanwhile, that the storm of critical controversy that broke over Craig's production was in some way prompted by his defiance of established, 'reactionary' practices. On the contrary, the revolutionary ideals of the new modernism had, by 1926, long since been implanted in the Scandinavian theatre.[4] Viggo Cavling, reviewing *The Pretenders* in *Politiken* (15 November 1926), succinctly characterises the true cause of critical dissatisfaction with Craig's ill-fated experiment:

> We have nothing against the simplification and stylization which Mr. Craig advocates, and we agree with him completely that the old-fashioned theatre art is often offensively glossy. But if one wants to stylize, one cannot stylize in general, but only within the framework and tone and milieu in which the play takes place – as Max Reinhardt and Jessner have done time and time again, with sublime results. And the Craigian method could undoubtedly have been applied with success here, if only the coldness of the North, the harshness of the Middle Ages, the darkness of Catholicism had been allowed to come through. Instead, we were given scenery composed of parti-coloured blocks, Italian banners, French ribbon backdrops, Japanese lanterns, oriental gates, and so on.

Critic after critic reiterated the same basic objection: although Craig's diaphanous stage pictures might seem 'like a multi-coloured cloud', the impression they conveyed 'had nothing to do with that bit of the Norwegian Middle Ages to which Henrik Ibsen has sought to convey us'.[5] It seemed to more than one reviewer that Craig's scenery and costumes

> reminded one of the staging of *The Countess Cathleen*. *The Pretenders* was served up as though it were an Irish saga, and not a ponderous Nordic drama of destiny partaking of all the violence of the Middle Ages, its proud spirit torn to pieces in the conflict

between the wildness of heathendom and the Christian sense of guilt. No, Gordon Craig, regardless of how sophisticated he may be, is unable with his aestheticized designs to express that Nordic tone which pervades the play. To see *Peer Gynt* in Paris is bad, but to see Gordon Craig in Copenhagen is – in a Nordic Drama – even worse.[6]

Even Svend Borberg, ardent champion of the new modernism and one of Craig's most enthusiastic partisans, was obliged to concur that

> this is surely not *Ibsen*! . . . This is an Irish tale, yes exactly Irish – undoubtedly Craig has Irish blood in his veins, as do all Englishmen with imagination, and this reminds us, both in its ecstatic style and especially in its colour harmonies, of the miniatures of the Irish monks, of Yeats's *Countess Cathleen*, of red hair, green peasants' coats – wonderful, but why use it for Ibsen![7]

'The Royal Theatre ought to invite Mr. Craig to stage a Shakespeare production', Cavling's review went on to observe. 'Here, there would be no prefixed limitations on his imaginative impulse toward experimentation. In the Nordic drama he seems too much a foreigner.' In other words, the point being urged here is that Ibsen's historical plays conjure up a tangible and localised world (which does *not* mean a parochial one) that is not adequately served by the same abstract, dematerialised style of production that Shakespeare's plays (or even less concretely localised Ibsen dramas like *Brand* or *Peer Gynt*) might seem to admit or even to invite. Obviously, the demand in 1926 was not for a return to an outmoded *trompe l'oeil* illusionism. Craig's right in general to seek his inspiration in the tone and spirit of the play itself, rather than in the poet's stage directions, was not in any way being challenged by the Copenhagen critics – only his failure to conceive an original theatrical image which effectively projected the concretely Nordic and medieval tone and spirit of the *specific* play before him ('that dreadfully difficult play for intellectuals', as he rather unsympathetically termed it). The point has significant wider implications for Craig's art as a whole, but it also draws attention to a dilemma that must be confronted in any re-interpretation of Ibsen's early romantic dramas on the modern stage.

(That this dilemma still seems very much with us today was

illustrated by the first professional American production of *The Pretenders*, presented by the Guthrie Theater in 1978 as its contribution to the Ibsen sesquicentennial. Alvin Epstein's 'Shakespearean' *mise-en-scène*, determined chiefly by the demands of the Guthrie's open thrust stage, utilised massive, moveable set components, at once rough-hewn and intricately carved, which suggested to the Minneapolis reviewers 'the barbaric guts and the increasing refinement of this transitional period. Carved monoliths opened into church doors'. Period costumes of rough, heavy homespun added to the critics' impression of 'a dark-hued medieval ambience filled with deft touches of illumination'. Underlying all this impressive solidity, one senses a *rétardataire*, Meininger-like determination to – in the words of a lengthy programme declaration soliciting financial contributions – 'present you with a slice-of-life from centuries ago' and 'to increase your enjoyment by making props and set-pieces seem more startlingly realistic. . . . We value authenticity at the Guthrie because we know it adds a special dimension to every play'.)

II

After he left Norway in 1864, Ibsen entered a distinct new phase in his artistic development. Both *Brand* and *Peer Gynt*, the first two plays which he completed during his long, voluntary exile, were conceived as dramatic poems, unfettered by the technical limitations of the theatre because they were intended, initially at least, for a reading public. It remained for the versatile Swedish director Ludvig Josephson to recognise the immense theatrical potential of the monumental reading dramas, and his pioneering stage version of *Peer Gynt*, seen for the first time at Christiania Theatre early in 1876, stretched the resources of the theatre of pictorial illusion to the very limit. His flamboyantly colourful *mise-en-scène*, enhanced by a commissioned score composed by Edvard Grieg (from which the play has never fully succeeded in extricating itself), presented Peer's progress as a series of striking (if rather literalised) pictorial effects. When the play finally reached the Copenhagen stage fully ten years later, in a production at Dagmar Theatre directed by its manager Theodor Andersen, this romantic, pictorialised style of presentation still seemed the only reasonable alternative. The mammoth Dagmar production, in which Grieg again assisted personally and for which the Norwegian star Henrik Klausen re-created his playful and distinctly lyrical interpretation of Peer, has attracted a certain amount of critical attention because Ibsen himself contributed detailed written advice about the performance and later expressed his approval of it.[8] In turn, the emphasis, so evident in this production, on the creation of a colourful and vivid but fundamentally believable stage picture was to maintain its influence on the stage history of *Peer Gynt* for decades to come. (For the more simplified and suggestively dematerialised approach that such a work actually seems to demand, *Peer Gynt*, like Strindberg's later dream plays, would have to wait until the post-naturalistic period.)

At Dagmar Theatre in 1886, however, the implicit objective was to produce an unmitigated conviction of 'reality' in sets, costumes, and lighting – a reality remarkable at once for its 'authentic' ethnographic flavour and for its intensely picturesque appeal. Edvard Brandes regarded the production as being 'of great significance' precisely because 'it peels off, so to speak, the play's outward symbolism and reveals Ibsen's work as a poem about our own lives'.[9] This nineteenth-century *Peer Gynt* made little effort to distinguish between the realms of the real and the unreal, nor did it concern itself, as a modern production inevitably would, with the articulation of a web of symbolic resonances in the work. Thirty-nine actors were utilised and hence some doubling occurred – but purely on practical rather than on thematic or psychoanalytic grounds (as, for instance, in a recent, remarkable Danish production at Aarhus Theatre in which Aase and Solveig, Peer's mother and beloved, were played by the same actress). Even the fantastic and grotesque elements in the Dagmar performance – the trolls, elves, and goblins whom Peer encounters in the Hall of the Mountain King – were made to appear as 'real', in the context of their own world, as Mother Aase, Solveig, and the revellers at Hægstad farm did in theirs. Rather than being seen as inhabitants of a symbolic and intensely disturbing dream world, they were 'entertainingly grotesque' figures (to borrow Brandes' description) modelled on the familiar elves of the *eventyr* tradition of adventure and romance – a tradition of which the plays and tales of H. C. Andersen, or the folk ballets of August Bournonville, or, for that matter, an early Ibsen play like *Midsummer Eve* all partake.

For the creation of this four-and-one-half hour spectacle the play was shortened to eighteen scenes, each one of which depended on a suitably atmospheric setting and hence required a correspondingly complicated scene change. Both the director's notes and Ibsen's own remarks and cuts are preserved in a surviving promptbook that amply demonstrates an abiding preoccupation with credible characters and situations and with a 'factual' vision of a recognisably Norwegian context. In the opening scene, for example, Peer placed his angry, shouting mother atop the roof of a solidly three-dimensional replica of a Norwegian log cabin. (A charming drawing by Ibsen, depicting Peer taking off at full speed after having performed this feat, is accompanied by the playwright's characteristically precise and eminently practical suggestions for accomplishing it.) Aase's death (which in so many productions has proven to be the drama's death as well!) was played in a comparably 'authentic' reproduction of a 'simple Norwegian room', corresponding closely to Ibsen's stage directions ('a log fire burns and illuminates the chimney; a cat on a chair by the foot of the bed'). Other of the play's Norwegian scenes were endowed with an even more boldly picturesque quality: Peer's newly-built cabin in the forest, decorated with reindeer's antlers above the doorway, was placed in the midst of a snowy landscape, and the faithful Solveig made her entrance in the scene exactly as Ibsen had envisioned it in his text – on skis! (Such an effect, unusual though it might seem, presented no particular problem for a nineteenth-century director or designer who knew his craft. The promptbook informs us how it was done: 'To the right [of Peer's cabin] a long track with blocks, to which are fastened a pair of skis with bindings. . . . Solveig steps out of these as soon as the blocks reach the ground.')

These realistic indications of a concrete milieu and culture were, of course, juxtaposed with the more exotic and spectacular effects that were to be found throughout – in the whimsically balletic episode in the Hall of the Mountain King, in the romantic tableaux that documented Peer's fourth-act adventures in the Morocco desert, and, not least, in the dramatic shipwreck scene which opened the final act, in which the vessel carrying a now aged Peer Gynt back to Norway founders and he saves himself (at the expense of the hapless Cook) by clinging to the keel of an overturned dinghy. For the wreck scene, a gauze scrim across the proscenium opening created the atmosphere of a foggy, storm-tossed night on the North Sea. The entire stage floor around the ship was covered with a large 'sea cloth', beneath which 'wave-boys' – whose job was to facilitate the disappearance of the vessel, and whose energetic movements also created the illusion of a violently agitated sea – were deployed.

'When the ship sinks [into a large trap in the stage floor],' notes the promptbook, 'the mast falls and the sea cloth is pulled over the trap' by these unseen stagehands. The 'singular realism' and the 'shattering effect' for which the shipwreck scene was praised by the critics drew additional strength from Grieg's turbulent introduction to the last act, 'a very stirring tone painting', in the words of the music critic for *Politiken* (16 January 1886), which presented 'the whole orchestra . . . in agitation, whining like the howling storm, raging with muffled reverberations'.

The 'romantic' conception of *Peer Gynt* which the Dagmar production so vividly exemplifies is inextricably bound up with Grieg's still famous and familiar score. The richly melodious and nationalistic strains of Grieg's music inevitably endowed such a production with a basic tone of lyricism and sentimentality, casting over it an atmospheric aura of romance which largely ignored the ironic and anti-sentimental elements in Ibsen's conception of Peer – the poetic dreamer of dreams who is *also* the liar, the egoist, the self-deceiver, the man who shirks responsibility and shuns reality, determined instead to follow the easier course of 'going round-about'. Yet, more than half a century would pass before the conciliatory atmosphere of folklore and romance would cease to colour major revivals of *Peer Gynt* in Scandinavia. Eventually, a very crucial step in this direction was taken in 1948, when the Norwegian actor-director Hans Jacob Nilsen presented his controversial anti-romantic reinterpretation of the play, translated for the occasion into New Norse, at Det Norske Teatret in Oslo. As part of his programme to make people leave the performance 'shaken but fortified, much more aware of the power the trolls have over us but more prepared to fight them', Nilsen replaced Grieg's splendid but (one now felt) inappropriate romanticism with the stark, dissonant tones of a new score by Harald Sæverud (Opus 28), whose music attempted to create a coherent pattern of 'musical-psychological development' for the play. It was Ingmar Bergman, however, who ultimately conceived the bolder and simpler expedient of dispensing with the rival claims of Grieg and Sæverud alike. In his massive five-hour revival of *Peer Gynt* at the Malmö Stadsteater in 1957, the orchestral element was finally silenced and musical accompaniment was held to the absolute minimum required by the play – Solveig's song was sung to a Norwegian folk tune; Ingrid Thulin's Anitra gyrated to the stark accompaniment of a drum solo. The overall effect, reviewers declared, was 'astonishing; it is like seeing a

painting cleansed of its yellowed exhibition varnish'.[10] Enthusiasts
and sceptics alike agreed that here, at last, was 'Ibsen's poem
liberated in word and picture from the lyrical and musical
paraphernalia of theatrical tradition'.[11]

'For us,' declared the programme for Bergman's ambitious
renewal, 'the essential thing has been to present the work as it is,
without expressionistic trappings and topical political pointers but
also without wrapping it in a romanticism which it had broken with
at its very inception.' The aim of this epoch-making, ninety-actor
production – which may be seen as the outstanding example in
Scandinavia of the anti-illusionistic, de-romanticised, conceptual
approach that has, in a variety of different ways, come to
characterise modern stage interpretations of this Ibsen play – was
thus to cleanse both Ibsen's drama and its central character of all
the sentimental associations, poetic stereotypes, and conciliatory
idealisations that had accumulated about them over the years – and
to do so before the very eyes of the audience.[12] Instead of presenting
Peer Gynt as a kaleidoscopic series of more or less lifelike scenes, the
entire visual framework of this production was subordinated to a
single, ruling directorial concept – that of the play as a drama of
pilgrimage, of the inward, spiritual journey of Peer, the man who is
lost in illusions, towards disillusionment and nothingness. In order
to articulate this idea, Bergman gradually and very deliberately
removed the various decorative physical elements from his stage as
the action progressed. The action of the earlier scenes was
pictorially supported by a mixture of solid realistic details and
stylised back projections of black-chalk landscape sketches created by
Härje Ekman. For example, the wedding celebrations at Hægstad
farm took place in a basically realistic setting, framed by a vaguely
sinister and threatening vision of mountains in the background – a
vision which symbolically emphasised the predominantly anti-
idyllic tone that informed Bergman's interpretation of this wedding
scene as a raucous, noisy, drunken brawl which culminates in the
raw brutality of Peer's abduction of the bride. As the play moved on,
however, a development toward greater and greater simplification
and dematerialisation of the stage environment became evident. Projections alone were now used to establish, in a non-
representational manner, the prevailing scenic atmosphere, until,
by the end of the play, these too had been eliminated and the stage
was left completely stripped and empty. In the last act, all theatrical
paraphernalia had vanished; the immense stage at Malmö now

became an apparently endless, black, and vacant space that accentuated the old man's spiritual impasse and intensified his isolation and despair as he roamed about near the last crossroads of life, unable now to fantasise himself away from the reality and finality of death. In the darkness of the void, Peer encountered figures of an obviously and entirely symbolic character, who threatened him with doom and final extinction in the Button Moulder's casting ladle. The concluding moments of the play thus resolved themselves on a bleak and extremely subdued note of loneliness and of ultimate reckoning. Every trace of sentimentality was expunged from Peer's reunion with Solveig. The final picture which confronted the audience was that of 'only two human beings on an immense stage, and in the background the mute, bent figure of the Button Moulder with his ladle'.[13]

The strong visual expressiveness that is a hallmark of all of Bergman's stage productions is nowhere more striking than in the mass scenes which he created for his *Peer Gynt*. The intensely coloured scene in King Brose's troll court was virtually a Hieronymus Bosch vision of hell, with the trolls 'grouped like grotesque, animal-like creatures carved into the very mountain walls'.[14] In this episode, which took on the character of a sinister amplification of the preceding raucous festivities at Hægstad, the restless and optimistic Peer of Max von Sydow seemed literally on the verge of being swallowed up by creatures that rolled forward in a block 'like an infestation of vermin, fluttering and waving in uniform reactions until it breaks up, like an avalanche of lava-coloured rocks, and sucks itself firmly around [him], a sticky mass of hair and snouts'.[15] The sheer visual force of this scene lent it a nightmarish quality that continued to persist throughout the performance. This sense of nightmare recurred again and again – in Peer's horrified brush with the great, amorphous presence of the Boyg; in Anitra's writhing contortions before him in the desert; most of all, in his Kafkaesque encounter in the Cairo madhouse with a collection of 'staring, yawning, half-sleeping, aimlessly revolving and grimacing monsters dressed in the same khaki-coloured institutional outfits'.[16]

'The theatre calls for nothing,' Ingmar Bergman is fond of insisting. 'T.V. includes everything, film includes everything, there everything is shown. Theatre ought to be the encounter of human beings with human beings and nothing more. All else is distracting.' Herein, he continues, lies 'the *whole* secret of the theatre' – 'nothing more is needed than the slightest, simplest suggestion'.[17] But to this conviction, so effectively demonstrated in his *Peer Gynt*, one must add another cardinal precept from Bergman's theatre poetics: 'I cannot and will not direct a play contrary to the author's intentions. And I have never done so. Consciously. I have always considered myself an interpreter, a re-creator.'[18] If it might be argued that the earliest productions of *Peer Gynt*, by directors such as Josephson and Theodor Andersen, concentrated their efforts on a literal, virtually cinematographic rendering of the lyrical and romantic elements evident chiefly in the first and third acts of the play, and if a modern reformer like Hans Jacob Nilsen can be seen as turning his attention, and ours, to the psychological implications of the uglier and more grotesque elements (the trolls) in the second act, then Bergman's contribution has been to attempt a coherent and unifying interpretative image of the total play – one which penetrates beyond the limits of its first three acts into the dark and terrifying dimension of the work's final movement. And no production of Ibsen's Faust drama that fails to come to terms with the last act's spirit of existential isolation and spiritual suffering and atonement can justly be called truly coherent or complete.

III

By the end of the 1870s, of course, Ibsen had emerged from his 'poetic' period and had begun to forge an entirely new and different mode of dramatic expression – a mode that translated the stifling atmosphere of contemporary prejudices and bourgeois moral hypocrisy into a metaphor for an all-enshrouding tragic fate. Ibsen's 'modern' plays, which transformed the apparently neutral language and settings of the realistic style to create a new kind of dramatic poetry, redefined the nature of drama itself, and in turn they fired the imaginations of theatrical innovators across the face of Europe. In Scandinavia, the challenge of a style that took 'real life and exclusively that as the basis and point of departure'[19] was taken up without hesitation – and largely without the attendant controversy and scenes of moral outrage that accompanied the Ibsen movement in England or America – by a generation of important naturalistic directors that included August Lindberg in Sweden, Bjørn Bjørnson in Norway, and William Bloch in Denmark. Among these, Bloch in particular became the outstanding exponent of a naturalistic tradition in the Scandinavian theatre fully comparable to the more widely discussed 'revolutionary' advances being made elsewhere in Europe at this time.

Bloch's pioneering production of *An Enemy of the People* at the Royal Theatre in Copenhagen in March 1883 had firmly established the new style of stage naturalism in Scandinavia.[20] Two years later, his production of *The Wild Duck* at the same theatre provided even more eloquent testimony to the power of a style of Ibsen interpretation that would continue to maintain its influence on the Scandinavian theatre for the next half a century or more. 'The effect of [Ibsen's] art is doubly potent when brought to life on the stage', declared *Dags-Telegrafen* (24 February 1885), and most reviewers of Bloch's newest success agreed. His method, which emphasised the credible fabric of Ibsen's play through meticulous attention to carefully observed details and reactions taken from daily life, was a direct response to the playwright's own urgent affirmation that 'in both the ensemble acting and in the stage setting, this play demands truth to nature and a touch of reality in every respect'.[21] As such, however, this approach sought neither to neglect nor to obscure the mesh of powerful symbolic and poetic resonances beneath the tangible surface of *The Wild Duck*. As a director, Bloch was keenly responsive to Ibsen's subtle subtextual dramaturgy, and hence the emphasis he laid on significant, concrete details was never an end in itself but always a means – later to be adopted by other naturalistic directors from Antoine to Otto Brahm and Stanislavski – of achieving an evocative inner authenticity. In Bloch's aesthetic (as indeed in Ibsen's) the attention to the outer dimension of unmistakably truthful detail served a far more important purpose than that of merely chronicling reality or creating a deceptively lifelike impression. This attention was viewed as a strategy for deepening the audience's perception of the essential spirit and meaning of the play – for revealing an inner world within the apparently prosaic context of everyday life. 'The inanimate, material objects and the so-called lifelike touches were his means of illuminating and breathing life into the setting, the situation, the stage action – of creating the necessary atmosphere around the only true reality in art, that of the soul,' writes one observer about Scandinavia's foremost exponent of stage naturalism in the age of Ibsen.[22]

Bloch's very faithful but adroitly amplified renderings of Ibsen's two stage environments in *The Wild Duck* – Haakon Werle's richly and comfortably furnished study in Act 1, with its spacious and

elegant sitting room adjoining it, and Hjalmar Ekdal's contrast-
ingly simpler studio, with its strangely evocative inner loft –
became, with their solid walls, carefully selected furnishings, and
subtle changes of lighting, uncompromising, truthful comments on
the lives and actions of their inhabitants. The multitude of concrete
details incorporated by this director were not introduced simply for
their picturesque, decorative value; nor were they a result of the
essentially romantic sort of taste for local colour and ethnographic
accuracy which was to permeate the Dagmar Theatre *Peer Gynt*. In
Bloch's interpretation, stage setting served a much more central and
integral dramatic purpose. It was utilised to enrich and intensify the
particular mood and atmosphere of the play, to function as a visual
embodiment and crystallisation of its thematic architecture. As
such, the scenic environment became animated and charged with
an independent expressive potential of its own. 'When I walk into
the auditorium at night after the curtain has gone up,' Bloch liked to
remark, 'the atmosphere upon the stage should make me feel the
same as any guest walking into a strange parlour – the kind of house
it is, the kind of people there, and what goes on between them,
before I even step inside.'[23]

However, Bloch's special ability as an Ibsen interpreter extended
beyond his talent for creating a solid and convincing physical
environment in which the characters of the drama were seen to live
a life of their own. In addition, he used an evocative mosaic of
details to open up further vistas that lay just beyond the audience's
range of vision. The impingement of aspects of the environment
which lie on the periphery of what is actually shown on the stage is,
as we know, a device which is used to great effect in many of Ibsen's
plays. In *The Wild Duck*, the mood created by the setting was
suggestively expanded by Bloch to embrace those other rooms in the
play – the office into which Old Ekdal is admitted at the beginning
and from which he later emerges, a seedy and improbable interloper
in an ostensibly festive gathering; the dining room in which the
dinner is being held in the opening scene; and, above all, the
mysterious Ekdal attic – which are not directly visible but which are
painstakingly developed in his detailed promptbook.[24]

In particular, Bloch's *mise-en-scène* exploited to the utmost the
special character of the Ekdal milieu in order to project and sustain
an intense sense of dramatic mood. Hjalmar's studio, which
reviewers of the production agreed was 'a splendid setting, full of
atmosphere in the different lights in which it appears . . . and a

striking frame, spacious but desolate, around the life of the Ekdal family',[25] was furnished by the director with his customarily painstaking attention to fine nuances. 'The people in the play are completely new, and where would we get by relying on old theatrical clichés', August Lindberg, Bloch's Swedish counterpart, had declared in a letter to Ibsen prior to the Stockholm première of *The Wild Duck*.[26] For Lindberg as for Bloch, the one means of eliminating such undesirable stereotypes was by endowing the performance with the vitality and conviction of life itself. Lindberg's production of the play at Dramaten, which opened almost a month before Bloch's, had already caused something of a sensation with its microscopically truthful depiction of the Ekdal environment. The actors in his performance moved in convincing naturalistic fashion among the furnishings, handling props that possessed the solidity and authenticity of observed reality. The door frames were solid, the doors boasted real door-knobs, and there was even a much-discussed night-commode, complete with chamber pot, which offered a visually eloquent comment of its own on the Ekdal milieu. In Bloch's production, meanwhile, the major source of fascination seemed to be his treatment of the large, irregularly shaped interior loft at the back of Hjalmar's studio – a striking physical embodiment of the drama's shadowy atmosphere of fantasy, lies, and self-deception, at once real and weirdly unreal in its appearance. Filled by Bloch with an intriguing assortment of disparate objects – packing cases, a pair of geographical globes, hampers, a table, an old dresser piled with large books, several photographs of large groups of anonymous people, a dead pine tree – this mysterious loft, seen only in fleeting glimpses during the course of the play, exuded its own particular atmosphere of a dead and haphazardly constructed past. Then, among all these mouldering and inanimate objects in the attic, Bloch placed a small handful of live pigeons and chickens, in order to convey an impression of the living creatures that have their abode there and play their unwitting but essential part in the escapist fantasies of Ibsen's dreamers. Such a characteristically naturalistic touch was designed to strengthen a tangibly perceived atmosphere that rendered this specific domestic milieu believable and comprehensible – not only to the audience but also to the actors, who were thereby enabled to 'live' their roles with greater psychological conviction.

Such 'touches' were, however, never conceived by Bloch as merely striking but isolated flourishes in a picturesque *tableau vivant*.

Each detail contributed its share to an organic totality which he regarded as the ultimate goal of the director – a psychologically motivated integration of the play's complex character relationships into what he termed 'the inspired life of the ensemble'. His promptbook for *The Wild Duck* contains not only set descriptions, floor plans, and intricately planned patterns of movement, but also circumstantial instructions about stage business clearly intended to amplify, but not change, the integral *mise-en-scène* woven into the play by Ibsen himself. Throughout the performance attention was invariably concentrated upon a continually varied but relaxed and fluid pattern of action and movement, intended to create a natural impression. The judicious introduction of physical actions, in Stanislavski's sense of utilising stage objects for the purpose of endowing the scene with the conviction of reality, bonded the individual characters to their environment and lent the production its peculiarly dynamic and kinetic character. Running behind and beneath the flow of the dialogue, these activities served to integrate the individual figures into a fabric of human interrelationships, thereby making the pattern that underlies their related actions – the wounded struggle for survival – more coherent and more meaningful. Gina and Hedvig busied themselves with domestic activities – tidying the house, sewing, serving (real) food, reading, and, of course, retouching photographs. Hjalmar Ekdal, mournfully playing on his flute, was conceived by Emil Poulsen in the very terms in which Ibsen had described him, as a blend of essential naivety and lightly melancholy charm and warmth, a bit pretentious, a bit self-centred. The high point of this production and the pivotal point in Bloch's ensemble, however, was unquestionably Olaf Poulsen's memorable portrayal of Old Ekdal – a role which, in the hands of the greatest comic actor of his age, succeeded magically in fusing intensely human proportions with immense symbolic weight. His comings and goings with (real) hot water for that toddy which is his defence against the terror of reality, and his energetic hunting and rabbit-shooting in the attic made Olaf Poulsen's figure seem 'tragic and comic at the same time' – the craggy, grotesque focus of this picture of drifting, foundering humanity, 'the most perfect conceivable archetype of a man who has in every way suffered shipwreck in life'.[27]

In spite of the forceful impact of the individual acting performances in this production, however, the essential strength of William Bloch's directorial approach to Ibsen's drama resided, ultimately, not in its separate details but in its vigorous totality. Rather than isolate a single motif or choose a single mood for emphasis, Bloch deliberately accentuated the density of Ibsen's dramatic texture, the complexity of the pattern of interwoven and mutually sustaining themes and character relationships. The suggestive power and expressiveness of his interpretation of *The Wild Duck* derived from the *accumulated* effect of a multiplicity of fine points, a mosaic of nuances in the setting, the lighting, and the psychological shadings of character interpretations blended into the interaction of the ensemble. The subtle fusion of all these ingredients lent this textbook example of stage naturalism its distinctive character and life and bestowed upon it an added dimension of evocative, intensified dramatic atmosphere.

IV

In contrast to an earlier work like *Peer Gynt*, which has continued to foster new and imaginative reinterpretations in the modern theatre (one need only recall the 1971 agit-prop production by Peter Stein and the Schaubühne am halleschen Ufer, in which Peer, played by six actors, became a petit bourgeois deluded by false capitalistic values!), *The Wild Duck* and Ibsen's other major prose plays have tended to elicit less in the way of free-wheeling formal experiments based on symbolic design concepts, drastically stylised costumes, or expressionistic lighting effects. Reinforced as each of these plays is by the precisely detailed *mise-en-scène* which Ibsen himself has written into it, the style of theatrical representation initially evolved by Bloch and his contemporaries has, with some obvious modifications, continued to influence revivals of them throughout the present century. When Norway's Nationaltheatret presented its famous revival of *The Wild Duck* in 1949, for example, Halvdan Christensen's 'intricately detailed, intimately realistic' production exemplified a quietly intense style of performance which 'unobtrusively and objectively placed the milieu for the action in the decade to which it belongs, and which let real, everyday people remain real, everyday people, with dialogue that remains everyday speech without undue emphasis on profound pauses and vague symbolic images'.[28] Nor can it be said that productions of Ibsen's final 'symbolic' works have differed remarkably in this regard. In a revival of *The Master Builder* at Dramaten in 1937, starring Anders de Wahl as Solness and Harriet Bosse as his wife Aline, de Wahl's production skilfully incorporated the 'period' quality of the environment into his interpretative concept. The interiors he created for Solness's office and living room revealed, writes Agne Beijer, 'how he had revelled in creating a realistic *regie* of the eighties; every piece of furniture was as realistic as it was ugly. And there he himself stood, heavy and coarse in that massive bourgeois milieu which Solness has built around himself and to which he has never adjusted'.[29] In our own day, the impressive series of productions with which Norway's Nationaltheatret marked the playwright's sesquicentennial (specifically *Ghosts*, *Lady from the Sea*, and an intimate studio production of *Little Eyolf*) demonstrated once again the significance of coming to terms with the Ibsen tradition and absorbing it, rather than dismissing it out of hand, when attempting to shape a more 'modern' and relevant approach to his plays in the theatre. For, as one critic of these performances has observed,

> no matter how many torpedoes Ibsen may plant under the ark in *Ghosts* – society, marriage, the family, ideals, sexual and ethical codes, all of these are blown to bits! – this entire play is still placed within the framework of the naturalistic parlour which a whole century of theatre audiences have known as a symbol of security. This has been the playwright's chance: he was radical and revolutionary without rendering the theatre rootless. He never operates in a vacuum. He creates a tradition and yet is still part of a tradition.[30]

This is certainly not meant to suggest, however, that Ibsen's prose plays somehow remained utterly impervious to the anti-naturalistic ideals and innovative devices of the new modernism. Quite the contrary: from the startling experimental design work of Edvard Munch at the beginning of this century to the stylised productions of Ingmar Bergman in recent years, we find evidence of the eclectic but persistent search by Scandinavian designers and directors for an alternative to the naturalistic manner of staging Ibsen's 'modern' plays – an alternative arising out of the desire for a much more sharply defined conceptual approach to the plays, shaped by the New Stagecraft's triple goal of simplification, stylisation, and suggestion.

One important aspect of the new modernism, inspired largely by its distaste for the alleged 'drabness' of stage naturalism, was the renewed emphasis which it placed upon the role of the designer as an artist enjoying equal standing with the director. Out of this conviction arose the historic invitation which Max Reinhardt extended to Munch, Scandinavia's foremost painter during the Ibsen era, to create a series of designs for *Ghosts* in 1906. For this production, which opened Reinhardt's Kammerspiele in Berlin (and in which the director himself appeared as Engstrand), Munch devised an extraordinarily evocative setting which not only lent the performance its distinctive visual tone and texture, but also shaped the entire directorial image of the play decisively. By deliberately transferring the drama from the realm of reality to an imaginative level at which poetic and atmospheric values become far more emphatic than any of the earlier naturalistic productions had attempted to make them, the Munch-Reinhardt experiment opened the eyes of contemporary critics to an entirely 'new' Ibsen. Instead of confronting the audience with a physical environment consisting of a complex filigree of realistic details, in which no individual element was given particular emphasis, Munch's expressively simplified living-room setting for *Ghosts* stressed certain specific visual motifs, designed to heighten and deepen the interpretation of the work as a drama of destiny, rather than of character or psychology. In this interpretation the precise, logically ordered mosaic of reality – Ibsen's objectively rendered environment – was de-emphasised in order to intensify and render transparent certain predominant themes. In doing so, however, the contours of external reality were not distorted in an expressionistic manner; rather, reality was painted in a particularly revealing light and given a specific colouring in order to project an imaginative vision of the inner rhythms and tensions of the play. Dominated visually by a large, black chair – an object which seemed to Reinhardt to epitomise the sombre mood of the entire drama[31] – Munch's room, held in dark tones of reddish brown, black, grey, and violet, virtually exuded a heavy atmosphere of joylessness and constriction. In the background a sharply outlined mountain range which, in a vaguely threatening way, almost obscured the view of the sky heightened the feeling of imprisonment that communicated itself, almost with Strindbergian intensity, throughout the performance. As the past into which the characters are helplessly locked is at last fully revealed, the sinister shadows that hover in Munch's designs sprang to life, ruthlessly pursuing and engulfing the human figures on the stage. 'In the last, despairing moments of the play,' Julius Bab tells us, while the darkness was gradually pierced by the penetrating, cold grey shafts of the dawn before sunrise, 'as Mrs Alving rushed behind her son, towards the lamp, shadows as high as houses cast on the walls accompanied her like pursuing demons.'[32]

From Munch's time to our own, Scandinavian designers and directors have continued to seek out and present exceptional alternatives, of more or less radically dematerialised nature, to the dominant naturalistic style that has remained the customary rule in producing Ibsen's major prose plays. In recent years, of course, Ingmar Bergman has given us boldly untraditional and psychologically expressive stage interpretations of two of these plays, *Hedda Gabler* (Dramaten, 1964) and *The Wild Duck* (Dramaten, 1972). In the former instance, Ibsen's detailed naturalistic interior, presided over by the portentous portrait of General Gabler, was replaced by an uncluttered, stark red room furnished with uncompromising simplicity – a mirror, a sofa, an armchair (with antimacassar!), a black piano – and bisected by a central screen (sometimes a door, sometimes a barrier in the central character's mind) which split the stage into two spheres of simultaneous action. While Ibsen's text (or at least a deliberately edited version of it) was played in the acting area on the audience's right, Bergman's exploration of the unspoken actions and emotions of the play was presented on its left. From the psychologically revealing opening tableau to the final moments when she removes her elegant, high-heeled shoes before her fastidious suicide, Hedda's restless omnipresence and silent eavesdropping added an entirely new, dream-like dimension to the spectator's conventional mode of perceiving the realistic action of this drama.

This essentially cinematic technique of juxtaposing actual scenes with exposed glimpses of peripheral or implied off-stage action – a technique which Bergman himself insists is 'the oldest theatre device that ever existed' and has 'not a whit to do with film'–found an even bolder application in his brilliantly crystallised interpretation of *The Wild Duck*. Here, Ibsen's fateful and fleetingly perceived interior loft, the rich image of the flight from reality and the abode of the wild duck, was transformed into a fantastic ghost-attic located between the audience and the stage. 'Without stage properties and with only the aid of the lighting and the art of the actors, Bergman creates, before the eyes of the audience, that fantasy world which Hjalmar and Old Ekdal have built up around themselves', writes one critic. 'Here rule the night and the dreams, in scenes of such intensity and poetry that I have never witnessed their like.'[33] Old

Ekdal, Hjalmar, or Hedvig entered the loft through a side door from the studio – with the interesting result that they did not thereby disappear from view but were instead seen to draw nearer to the spectator – and only the roofbeams reflected on the black background and the facial expressions of the actors themselves indicated where they were and what it was they saw. Old, dried-out Christmas trees were dimly perceptible on either side of the Ekdal interior, creating the impression that its 'waking reality' was indeed suspended in a void, 'an island in the sea of flight from reality'. The camera-like sharpness of Bergman's magic realism seemed to lay bare the inner essence of the characters, as though they were 'lit through to the bare skeleton. . . . Driven to its fullest consequence, realism becomes unreal. The X-ray vision suddenly exposes not living and vaguely contradictory human beings, but rather psychological constructs in a laser-sharp, two-dimensional projection.'[34] Yet even Bergman's unusual technique of presenting exposed and deeply revealing glimpses of silent characters and implied peripheral actions – moments of what he calls simple, concrete psychic 'suggestion' that together 'create a dimension'[35] – can be said to find an antecedent in William Bloch's evocative, metaphoric use of total stage space.

Yet neither Bergman in our day, nor Bloch in his, nor any of the other men and women of the theatre who have contributed to the historical chronicle and artistic quest that we have been sampling here should be looked upon as providing an ultimate 'answer' or expounding a conclusive 'solution' to the problem of staging Ibsen. Any formula, as Peter Brook so wisely reminds us, is 'inevitably an attempt to capture a truth for all time'. And truth in the theatre – especially in Ibsen's theatre – is always on the move.

NOTES

1. A fuller, illustrated discussion of this general subject was published by the authors as 'Ibsen's Theatre: Aspects of a Chronicle and a Quest', *Modern Drama*, XXI (December 1978), pp. 345–78.
2. Edward Gordon Craig, *A Production, being Thirty-two Collotype Plates of Designs prepared or realised for The Pretenders of Henrik Ibsen and produced at the Royal Theatre, Copenhagen, 1926* (Oxford, 1930), p. 16.
3. Edward Gordon Craig, *Towards a New Theatre: Forty Designs for Stage Scenes with Critical Notes by the Inventor* (London, 1913; reprinted New York, 1969), p. 51.
4. For further details, see Frederick J. Marker and Lise-Lone Marker, *The*

Scandinavian Theatre: A Short History (Oxford, 1975), pp. 204–28.

5. *Aftenbladet*, 15 November 1926. All translations are by the present authors.
6. *København*, 15 November 1926.
7. *Ekstra-Bladet*, 15 November 1926.
8. Cf. Robert Neiiendam, *Fra Kulisserne og Scenen* (Copenhagen, 1966), pp. 87–8, and Klaus Neiiendam, 'The Second Staging of *Peer Gynt*, 1886', *Theatre Research International*, 11 (February 1977), pp. 104–17. For further details on the collaboration between Grieg and Ibsen, see *The Oxford Ibsen*, ed. James Walter McFarlane, vol. 11 (London, 1972), pp. 502–4. The prompt-book and other pieces of evidence concerning this production are in the Danish Theatre Museum.
9. *Politiken*, 16 January 1886.
10. *Göteborgs Handels- och Sjöfartstidning*, 9 March 1957.
11. *Berlingske Tidende* (Copenhagen), 10 March 1957.
12. Henrik Sjögren, *Ingmar Bergman på teatern* (Stockholm, 1968), p. 189.
13. *Malmö Tidningen*, 9 March 1957.
14. *Politiken* (Copenhagen), 9 March 1957.
15. *Göteborgs Handels- och Sjöfartstidning*, 9 March 1957.
16. *Svenska Dagbladet*, 9 March 1957.
17. Quoted in Sjögren, pp. 310, 311.
18. Quoted in ibid., p. 293.
19. Ibsen in a letter to Sophie Reimers, 25 March 1887.
20. For further details on this production, see Lise-Lone Marker and Frederick J. Marker, 'William Bloch and Naturalism in the Scandinavian Theatre', *Theatre Survey*, xv (November 1974), pp. 85–104.
21. Letter to Hans Schrøder, 14 November 1884.
22. Henri Nathansen, *William Bloch* (Copenhagen, 1928), p. 48.
23. Quoted in Nathansen, p. 75.
24. Bloch's promptbook as well as the *Regieprotokol* and the *maskinmester* journal for this production are preserved in the Royal Theatre Library.
25. *Dagstelegrafen*, 24 February 1885.
26. *Ibsen: Letters and Speeches*, ed. Evert Sprinchorn (New York, 1964), p. 243.
27. *Berlingske Tidende*, 23 February 1885.
28. Agne Beijer, *Teaterrecensioner 1925–1949* (Stockholm, 1954), p. 546.
29. Ibid., p. 239.
30. Jens Kistrup, 'Den moderne Ibsen: en dramatiker for alle', *Berlingske Tidende*, 6 July 1978.
31. Cf. Ernst Stern, *Bühnenbildner bei Max Reinhardt* (Berlin, 1955), p. 39.
32. Julius Bab, *Das Theater der Gegenwart* (Leipzig, 1928), p. 126.
33. Leif Zern in *Dagens Nyheter* (Stockholm), 18 March 1972.
34. Tord Bæckström in *Göteborgs Handels- och Sjöfartstidning*, 18 March 1972.
35. Quoted in Sjögren, pp. 314–5.

5 Ibsen and Modern Drama

MARTIN ESSLIN

In the English-speaking world today Henrik Ibsen has become one of the three major classics of the theatre: Shakespeare, Chekhov and Ibsen are at the very centre of the standard repertoire, and no actor can aspire to the very first rank unless he has played some of the leading roles in the works of these three giants. Among this triad, Ibsen occupies a central position which marks the transition from the traditional to the modern theatre. While Ibsen, like all great dramatists who came after him, owed an immense debt to Shakespeare, Chekhov (who regarded Ibsen as his 'favourite writer')[1] was already writing under Ibsen's influence. Ibsen can thus be seen as one of the principal creators and well-springs of the whole modern movement in drama, having contributed to the development of all its diverse and often seemingly opposed and contradictory manifestations: the ideological and political theatre, as well as the introspective, introverted trends which tend towards the representation of inner realities and dreams.

Ibsen's first and most obvious impact was social and political. His efforts to make drama and the theatre a means to bring into the open the main social and political issues of the age shocked and scandalised a society who regarded the theatre as a place of shallow amusement. And Ibsen's position seems unique in the history of drama in that he seems to have been the only playwright who, in his lifetime, became the centre of what almost amounted to a political party – the *Ibsenites* who in Germany, England, and elsewhere appear in the contemporary literature as a faction of weirdly dressed social and political reformers, advocates of socialism, women's rights, and a new sexual morality (as in the Ibsen Club, in Shaw's *The Philanderer*). Again and again one can find, in the contemporary literature, the anxious father who inquires of his daughter about to introduce him to her fiancé-to-be whether by any chance the young

71

man reads Ibsen and Nietzsche, thus *revealing* himself to be a dangerous subversive element. And the fact that Ibsen had become the symbol and figurehead of what amounted to a counter-culture has had a very considerable influence on the subsequent fluctuations of his posthumous fame and the appreciation of his plays by both the critics and the public.

It was not Ibsen himself, who greatly disliked this development, but a number of his early critics, admirers, and followers–Shaw, Archer, Brandes, Gosse, and others–who formulated the doctrines of Ibsenism which persisted for a long time and indeed still persist, inasmuch as Shaw's *The Quintessence of Ibsenism* is still (and deservedly) read as a masterpiece of Shavian polemical writing. The effect of this phenomenon was that Ibsen could, for a long time, be regarded as a principally political playwright commenting on topical social and moral issues. As a result, when some of the main objectives of what had been regarded as his closest concerns had been attained (for example: women's suffrage, a more tolerant attitude to sexual conduct, and the rejection of religious intolerance) the view spread that Ibsen had outlived his fame and become thoroughly out of date. Brecht expressed this view in 1928 when he declared that Ibsen's *Ghosts* had become obsolete through the discovery of Salvarsan as a remedy against syphilis.[2] Yet the very fact that a playwright's work could be seen as having played a vital part in bringing about a change in public opinion and social attitudes had an immense effect on the status of drama as a medium of expression, and its status as an experimental laboratory for social thought and social change. As Brecht put it in 1939: 'The drama of Ibsen, Tolstoy, Strindberg, Gorki, Chekhov, Hauptmann, Shaw, Kaiser and O'Neill is an experimental drama. These are magnificent attempts to give dramatic form to the problems of the time.'[3] It will be noticed that Ibsen's name comes first in Brecht's list of the masters of the new kind of serious, experimental drama. And deservedly so: it was Ibsen who established that tradition, and proved that the theatre could be a forum for the serious consideration of the problems of the age. He is thus the founder and source of the whole strand of modern political and ideological theatre. Brecht himself, who developed a style of playwriting which radically rejected the convention of drama that Ibsen used, can thus be seen to have followed a trail blazed by Ibsen. And indeed, Brecht did acknowledge a direct indebtedness to Shaw who in turn was a professed follower of Ibsen.

This is one of the lines of descent of the contemporary drama we can clearly derive from Ibsen. It was Ibsen whose revolutionary impact and ultimate success showed that drama could be more than the trivial stimulant to maudlin sentimentality or shallow laughter which it had become – at least in the English-speaking world – throughout the nineteenth century.

It is usually assumed that the shock caused by Ibsen, and the furiously hostile reaction his early plays provoked, were due to this political and social subversiveness. But that is only one part of the truth. Another important cause of this virulent reaction by audiences and critics alike lay in the revolutionary nature of Ibsen's dramatic method and technique. This is an aspect which is far more difficult for us to comprehend today as we have become completely conditioned to precisely this then 'revolutionary' convention. Much of the fury directed at the time against Ibsen had nothing to do with his supposed obscenity, blasphemous views, or social destructiveness. What was criticised above all was his *obscurity* and *incomprehensibility*. Ibsen, it was said again and again, was a *mystificateur* who was obscure on purpose in order to mask the shallowness of his thinking, and whose dark hints and mysterious allusions were never cleared up in his plays. This view is perfectly expressed in a notice of *Rosmersholm* by Clement Scott in the London *Daily Telegraph* (19 February 1891):

> The old theory of playwriting was to make your story or study as simple and direct as possible. The hitherto accepted plan of a writer for the stage was to leave no possible shadow of a doubt concerning his characterisation. But Ibsen loves to mystify. He is as enigmatical as the Sphinx. Those who earnestly desire to do him justice and to understand him keep saying to themselves: granted all these people are egotists or atheists, or agnostics, or emancipated, or what not, still I can't understand why he does this or she does that.

The matter could not be put more clearly: in the then traditional convention of playwriting (a convention which, indeed, had existed from the very beginnings of dramatic writing) not only was every character labelled as either a villain or a hero, but was also – through soliloquies, asides, or confessions to a confidant – constantly informing the audience of his most secret motivations. The audience therefore did not have to deduce the motivations of the characters from their actions; they *knew* what their motivations were *before* they acted. Playgoers had been used to this convention for centuries. It was only when the demand for realism, of which the later Ibsen was the principal exponent, closed these windows into the inner world of the characters that the audience was faced with the problem of having to decide for themselves what the motivations of many of the characters' otherwise unexplained actions might be. No wonder that audiences unprepared for a manner of presentation that confined itself to the simulation of ordinary, everyday conversation, which hardly ever includes the full disclosure of hidden desires or deep motivations, could not make head or tail of what was supposed to be happening. Moreover, this development coincided in time with the discovery of the unconscious portion of the human psyche – the recognition that in most cases people do not even *know* their own motivations and could thus not express them even if the dramatic convention allowed them to do so. The modern convention of dramatic dialogue is, accordingly, diametrically opposed to the classical one. Now the art consists precisely in opening insights into the characters' unconscious motivations and feelings through the interstices between the most trivial everyday exchanges of small talk.

While Ibsen was by no means the only, or even the first, naturalistic playwright to apply this technique, he was certainly regarded as the most representative and also the most extreme in its application – quite apart from obviously being the greatest master practitioner of it in his own time. The introduction of this *principle of uncertainty* into drama certainly represents a fundamental revolution in dramatic technique, a revolution which is still with us and continues to dominate dramatic writing of all kinds, including the dialogue techniques of avant-garde cinema (as in the work of Robert Altman or John Cassavetes, where the dialogue is out of focus and overlaps so that no more than a general sense emerges). So far has this technique been developed that Ibsen now tends to appear to us over-meticulous and obvious in motivating his characters, however daring in breaking entirely new ground he might have appeared to his contemporaries. What is beyond doubt is that the line of development extends directly from Ibsen to Chekhov, who refined the technique of oblique or indirect dialogue and evolved the concept of the sub-text hidden beneath the explicit language of the dialogue, as well as to Wedekind who was the first to employ deliberately non-communicating dialogue so that the characters – too involved in themselves to listen to what their partners say – deliver what amounts to two monologues in parallel. And it is from Chekhov and Wedekind that the masters of contemporary non-communicating dialogue, such as Harold Pinter and Eugène Ionesco, can trace their ultimate descent.

To illuminate how direct this line of descent is, one has only to point out that James Joyce was not only an enthusiastic admirer of Ibsen in his youth but that he also wrote a very Ibsenite play – the much undervalued and neglected *Exiles* –which, in fact, makes this principle of uncertainty of motives its main theme. It is the subject raised in the final dialogue between Rosmer and Rebecca West in *Rosmersholm*: that one can, in fact, never know another human being's true motivation. Rosmer and Rebecca, because of the impossibility of any full and final awareness that the other's love is pure, can confirm their devotion to each other only in their willingness to die for love – whereas Richard Rowan, the highly autobiographical hero of Joyce's play, admits: 'I can never know, never in this world. I do not wish to know or to believe. I do not care. It is not in the darkness of belief that I desire you. But in restless, wounding doubt . . . ' Here this modern *principle of uncertainty* in human motivation is not only offered to the spectators, left in doubt about the characters' true feelings, but to the characters themselves whose love in fact is seen to spring directly from that very uncertainty; for full knowledge and total security would be an end-point, the beginning of stagnation and complacency and thus the death of love, which must constantly renew itself out of risk and uncertainty. It is no coincidence that Harold Pinter adapted this play and twice directed performances of it. His deliberate abandonment of supplying motivations of any kind to his characters in plays like *The Homecoming*, *Old Times* or *No Man's Land* might be regarded as continuing the practice of Joyce and thus, ultimately, of Ibsen.

Affinities and organic evolutionary links in technique between writers like Ibsen, Joyce, and Pinter also highlight the close connection between the technique and form of their work and its subject matter. The method of writing dialogue itself opens up the problem of human communication, motivation, and the nature of the personality – the self. Here too Ibsen stands at the very well-spring of modern literature. And even writers whose technique has very little in common with that of Ibsen are organically linked with him in this respect. James Joyce, the dedicated Ibsenite, links Ibsen with another great writer of our time, Samuel Beckett – in spite of the fact that Beckett's anti-illusionist and non-realist techniques are diametrically opposed to those of Ibsen's plays. For, I venture to suggest, both Beckett and Ibsen are ultimately deeply concerned with a subject matter of fundamental modernity: the problem of *Being*, the nature of the self, with the question of what an individual means when he uses the pronoun *I*. How can the self be defined? Can one even speak of a consistent entity corresponding to an individual's self? This, it seems to me, is the fundamental and underlying subject matter of Ibsen's *oeuvre* which was masked, for his contemporaries, by its surface preoccupation with social and political questions. Moreover, it is this problem which links Ibsen's earlier poetic drama with his later prose plays.

Here again Ibsen's uncanny ability to reflect the main currents of thought of his time emerges; for the problem of human identity, the nature of the self, seems to derive directly from the decline of religious belief which was the mainspring of the intellectual upheavals and revolutions of the nineteenth century to which Ibsen's entire *oeuvre* responded. As long as man was deemed to have an eternal essence, a soul which had been especially created for him by God and destined to persist – in Heaven or Hell – for all subsequent eternity, there was no problem about the nature of human identity. Each individual was believed to have his own special character and potential, which he might or might not fully develop to its utmost realisation, but which eventually would emerge into eternity. Swedenborg saw each individual in *Heaven and Hell* as bearing the outward form and features of his or her deepest nature. It was with the loss of transcendental beliefs of this nature that human identity became a problem. Was man the chance product of his genetic inheritance or of his environment? And if so, what was the true inner core of his self, its permanent component, as against the multitude of contradictory impulses which at any moment pull him in this or that direction?

Ibsen, although he insisted that he read few books and confined himself to reading the newspapers right down to the advertisements, was a brilliant sounding-board for all the philosophical cross-currents of his time, whatever the means by which he might have become aware of them. Already the protagonists of *The Pretenders*, or Julian in *Emperor and Galilean*, reflect the problem of the self, the need to search for the self's real core, and the awareness that the realisation of one's true self is the highest human objective. Brand, who is torn between the abstract dictates of his faith on the one hand (a faith he experiences as an implacable imperative existing outside himself), and his impulsive human instincts towards his child and his wife on the other, brings this problem of identity into particularly sharp focus. So also does Peer Gynt, who realises that being sufficient to oneself (that is, merely living by one's contradictory, momentary, instinctive, sensual impulses) actually leads to failure in developing a self. The image of the onion with its core of nothingness is indeed very Beckettian, which is another way of saying 'existentialist'.

For the nothingness at the centre of our own perception of ourselves is, with Kerkegaard (whom Ibsen, even if he had never read him, must have understood intuitively from the climate of discussion around him) and with Sartre, precisely the realisation of human *freedom*. The scene, at the end of *The Lady from the Sea* where Ellida has to be given her total freedom by her husband before she can freely decide to commit herself to him, seems to me the perfect expression of the existentialist position in drama (rivalled only by another great and even earlier proto-existentialist play, Kleist's *Prince of Homburg*). Here a character, Ellida, finds her true self by an act of her own will. Self-realisation as the creation of an integrated self out of nothing – the mere welter of instinctive drives – is the way out of the despair engendered by the disappearance of the notion of a God-centred and pre-ordained selfhood. In the case of Ellida, her encounter with the Stranger had conjured up before her a *false self-image* dictated by her animal attraction to him. And here again we are in a very modern field of ideas, the idea of *false consciousness* – a self-image which could easily have become destructive by preventing the potential integration of the personality in a harmonious balance between conflicting drives and needs, just as Brand's and Julian's false self-images ultimately lead to their downfall, or as Peer Gynt's failure to transcend the mere indulgence of his sensuality probably does (for, surely, the final vision of Peer's return to Solveig is no more than a fantasy, a dream image). Ellida's decision to commit herself – in full freedom – to Wangel seems to provide her with a valid, workable and harmoniously integrated self which, however, still remains precarious and problematic.

It is curious that the part of the Stranger, that giver of a false and destructive self-image to Ellida is, in another play, *The Master Builder*, played by Ellida's own step-daughter – Hilda Wangel. There Solness has transmitted his own false (because self-deceptive) self-image to Hilda who, years later, returns to confront him with it and to demand its realisation in action. Here the problematic nature of the human self is posed in a particularly brilliant dramatic form: Solness is faced with the reflection of his own now certainly obsolete idea of himself (which was a falsehood even at the time when he implanted it in Hilda's mind) in a manner which is reminiscent of the way Krapp is brought to confront his former and falsely romantic self in Beckett's play *Krapp's Last Tape*. The dramatic techniques could not be more different, but in substance the two plays resemble each other very closely. In Ibsen's play it is Hilda's memory which plays the part of the tape-recorder in Beckett's bleakly economical recreation of the same situation.

False consciousness, deceptive self-images, the *I* experiencing itself as the *Not-I* (to quote a Beckettian expression which has become the title of one of his plays) – these are expressions of a twentieth century cluster of problems for which Ibsen had his own terminology: he called this syndrome the *Life-lie* or, in a different perspective, the *lure of the ideal*. Peer Gynt's self-indulgence is, in this context, akin to Hjalmar Ekdal's complacency and self-deception – and the destructiveness of commitment to an abstract ideal on the part of Gregers Werle, to Brand's rigidity in blindly following the dictates of an abstract, revealed faith. John Gabriel Borkman, who has sacrificed his capacity for love, his human sensuality, to a Napoleonic self-image to which he still clings long after it has lost all reality, puts the problem of the self to discussion as much as the figure of Rubek, who betrayed both his capacity for love and for real greatness as an artist by opting for the compromise of worldly success and wealth – Peer Gynt's sufficiency to one's baser impulses. Always there is a conflict between irreconcilable aspects of the self, which the individuals concerned have failed to integrate into an harmonious, well-balanced whole.

If one looks at the underlying theme of Ibsen's *oeuvre* in this way, his preoccupation with the problem of women's rights, which so scandalised his contemporaries, also appears in a different perspective: Ibsen himself repeatedly insisted that in writing *A Doll's House* he had not, basically, been concerned with feminism, but merely with the problem of Nora's self-realisation as a human being. If Hilda Wangel destroys Solness by imposing upon him the self-image of a conquering hero unafraid to ascend the highest tower, so Helmer has imposed upon Nora the degrading role and self-image of a child-wife; and in walking out of the marriage she merely – that seems to have been the point Ibsen was concerned with – asserts her human rights to fashion her own self-image and to create her own integrated self.

Conversely, in what I feel is Ibsen's most 'modern' play, *Hedda Gabler*, we are presented with a character whose self-realisation is made tragically impossible by a number of external factors beyond her control. Hedda is basically a creative personality who cannot realise her potential in a society which does not allow women to live as independent human beings, while her sexual drive towards Løvborg cannot come to fruition because her rigid conditioning by having been brought up as an upper-class lady makes it impossible for her to defy convention by becoming Løvborg's mistress (as Thea, who has not been so conditioned, does). Thus Hedda is trapped in a truly tragic dilemma. Her seeming wickedness results from the confusion and contradictions within her own self-image between, on the one hand, her need to reject the role into which her upbringing and society have forced her (the dutiful and middle-class housewife and mother-to-be) and, on the other, her inability to do so because of the strength of her conditioning and the pressure of public opinion. Her destructiveness is thus merely her creativeness gone wrong, her tragic failure to achieve true selfhood.

Sexuality, and especially female sensuality, which did not officially exist at all for the Victorians, was seen by Ibsen as one of the dangerous instincts insofar as its suppression by the demands of society forced the individual into false or inadequate integrations of his self. Mrs Alving's failure to break out of her marriage in *Ghosts* foreshadows Hedda Gabler's inability to give herself to Løvborg, and is shown by Ibsen to elicit similarly tragic results. In *Little Eyolf* the conflict is between motherhood and uninhibited female sensuality. Rita Allmers is the most openly sexually voracious character in Ibsen's plays: here the rejection of motherhood derives from an undue concentration on the sensual aspect of sex. The child is maimed because the mother neglected him while engaged in the sexual act; and Eyolf ultimately dies because his mother wishes him dead as an obstacle to her uninhibited indulgence of sexual activity. But Rita's exaggerated sexual drive may well spring from her husband's equally disproportionate commitment to his ideal, his work as a philosopher, which has led him to neglect both her sexual needs and their child's emotional and educational demands.

. Ultimately this problem of the self is that of the missing core of the onion, the ultimate nothingness at the heart of the personality, the absence of a pre-ordained integrating principle which would automatically harmonise the conflicting drives and instincts that propel the individual in a multitude of centrifugal, disintegrating directions. That is why self-realisation, the creation of such an integrating principle by an act of will has become the task which confronts all of Ibsen's heroes. Seen from this angle, the problem of guilt in a play like *Rosmersholm* also appears in a new and more contemporary light. Here the false solutions arrived at in the past, the false self-images they have created, come between the individual and the ultimate realisation of his or her true self-image. The tradition of the Rosmers is as stifling as the upper-class rigidities of General Gabler's family; and false concepts of duty, on the one hand, and Rebecca's admittedly selfish instinctive sexuality, on the other, create what to these characters must appear as a situation without a way out. Whether, as Freud suggested, Rebecca West felt guilty under the curse of Oedipus (just having learned that she had committed incest with her father) or whether she felt that she had attained to a love of such purity that she could not, under the pressure of Victorian ideas, contemplate its sexual consummation – these characters are trapped in veritable labyrinths of false consciousness.

These are the thematic elements in Ibsen's *oeuvre* which, in my opinion, not only link him to the main preoccupations of contemporary drama but also constitute his continued relevance to the concerns of our time.

There is, however, another aspect of his work which makes Ibsen peculiarly relevant to the dramatic literature of our time. Contemporary drama – whether it is the *epic theatre* created by Brecht; the *absurdist* strain represented by playwrights like Beckett, Genet, Ionesco, and Pinter; or the *documentary* strain of contemporary political theatre – is essentially anti-illusionist, anti-realistic (if realism is understood as the quasi-photographic reproduction of the external appearance of the phenomenal world). Ibsen is generally regarded as the antithesis of this position, as a realist, even a naturalist, who in the most influential phase of his activity strove for complete photographic verisimilitude: a world of rooms without a fourth wall.

This view of Ibsen is correct, up to a point. But Ibsen's essentially poetic genius also propelled him away from photographic realism. That there are dream-like elements, highly reminiscent of the introspective fantasy world of the Absurdists, in Ibsen's earlier plays, in *Brand* and *Peer Gynt*, that there is a vast epic sweep that transcends all realism in *The Pretenders* and *Emperor and Galilean*, is only too obvious. Again and again in these plays the action shifts from the external world into the protagonists' dreams or fantasies: the voice from the avalanche in *Brand*, the Troll scenes in *Peer Gynt*, Peer Gynt's shipwreck, the whole Button Moulder sequence and, indeed, the final vision of Solveig, are dreamlike projections of the characters' inner visions. When Ibsen made the decision to devote himself to realistic prose drama these dream and fantasy elements were – on the surface – suppressed. Yet they are continuously present, nevertheless. They emerge above all in what has come to be regarded as Ibsen's increasing resort to symbolism. Having renounced the use of *poetry in the theatre* (in the form of verse or grandly poetic subject matter) Ibsen made more and more use of *poetry of the theatre* which emerges from the sudden transformation of a real object into a symbol, from the metaphoric power of an entrance or an exit, a door opening or closing, a glance, a raised eyebrow or a flickering candle.

It is my contention – and conviction – that the continuing power and impact of Ibsen's plays spring from precisely this poetic quality. If we accept that all fiction, however realistic its form, is ultimately the product of the imagination, the fantasy-life, the daydreaming of its author, then even the most realistic drama can be seen, ultimately, as a fantasy, a daydream. The more creative, the more complex, the more original, the more poetic the imagination of the writer, the greater will be this element in his work. It is one of the hallmarks of the best work of some of our foremost contemporary playwrights that they are conscious of this position and make use of it. The plays of Edward Bond and Harold Pinter, to name but those who most readily come to mind, are examples of this tendency: they are conceived as working both on the level of extreme realism and at the same time on that of fantasy and dream. In this they have surely been anticipated by Ibsen. The continued and undiminished impact of even Ibsen's most seemingly political plays owes, in my opinion, a great deal to that immense hidden and mysterious power which springs from the co-existence of the realistic surface with the deep subconscious fantasy and dream elements behind it: the simulated forest wilderness in the attic of *The Wild Duck*, the white horses of *Rosmersholm*, the ghosts that haunt Mrs Alving, the mysterious Stranger of *The Lady from the Sea*, the spectral Rat Wife of *Little Eyolf*, Borkman's self-created prison, Løvborg's manuscript as Hedda's aborted dream-child, the haunting appearance of the destructive and seductive Hilda Wangel in *The Master Builder*, Aline's dolls in the same play – they all are powerful poetic metaphors, fantasy-images as well as real objects and forces which can be perceived in a sober, factual light.

For, ultimately, the power of all drama springs from its innermost poetic nature as a metaphor of reality, a representation of the whole of reality which of necessity must include the internal world, the world of the mind (both conscious and subconscious), as well as the external reality of rooms, furniture, and cups of coffee. As soon as that external reality is put on the stage it becomes, by the very nature of the theatrical phenomenon, an image, a metaphor of itself: *imaged*, imagined, and by that very fact a mental, a fantasy phenomenon. '*Alles Vergaengliche ist nur ein Gleichnis*', as Goethe puts it in the final scene of *Faust*: all our ephemeral, evanescent reality is itself, ultimately, merely metaphor, symbol.

It is this quality of the metaphorical power, the poetic vision behind the realistic surface of Ibsen's later plays – their impact as images, and the complex allusive representations of those aspects of human existence, those problems that lie beyond the expressive resources of merely discursive language – in which their real greatness and enduring impact lies. And these, precisely, are the elements in Ibsen which are both highly traditional as well as continuously contemporary, continuously modern.

NOTES

1. Letter to A. L. Vishnevski, 7 November 1903: 'You know Ibsen is my favourite writer . . . ', *The Life and Letters of Anton Tchekhov*, eds Koteliansky and Tomlinson (London, 1925), p. 293.
2. Brecht, *Gesammelte Werke*, VII, p. 143.
3. Ibid., p. 288.

6 *Hedda Gabler*: the Play in Performance

JANET SUZMAN

I am acutely aware that this play has been dissected brilliantly before. People of much spirit have written and talked about it with perspicacity and feeling. I am aware too of the jostling queue I stand in, *but* I caught the bus once and all I wish to do is to report part of the journey I took.

Actually, it occurs to me that *talking* about acting is a contradiction in terms. Gesture, tones of voice, expressions in the eye, movements of the body, all these are quite beyond me to describe in words. So where I may sound dogmatic, bear with me and remember that the assurance comes from the *experience*. And remember too that stage-time is ruthless and singular. Where I *dwell* here, I *flew* on the stage. A minute of exposition here is a south-sea of discovery there. Talking about the acting of *this* play in particular seems to me a positively perverse exercise. Because Hedda will not stand definition. Some nights, true to form, she eluded me as she will elude others. But that's her secret strength. *She* knew she could not be defined, the devil, and in the end she triumphs in that evasion. The free spirit roams in Hades.

Before I start, would you be good enough to bear in mind the following personal maxims of mine? I say this because you are, on the whole, a rather specialised audience to whom the acting process may be largely unfamiliar.

(i) You cannot act concepts or abstractions or theories. Freud may well have been right about Rebecca West's Oedipus complex, but you can't *act* an Oedipus complex.

(ii) What Ibsen meant I see *only* on the page of the text. It might seem blasphemous to say that if this play were by an anonymous author, mysteriously found in some attic, I should still be able to act it.

(iii) From the actor's viewpoint, realistic drama is not all that realistic. Never mind if they are dethroned, Millamant and Hedda are no less out of the ordinary than Cleopatra.

(iv) *All* drama deals with characters in a state of crisis. Ophelia comes on in a high old state of panic – and so does Hedda. There is no essential difference in kind.

(v) Acting is acting as a rose is a rose, be it in bare staccato prose or the most lyrical poetry. It requires the same concentration of forces to convey meaning in one word as it does in a line of iambics. The classical actor is simply one who has made the discovery that words are not frightening. On the contrary, they are his delight.

To examine a play of this calibre with any degree of thoroughness you spend, let us say, a month (preferably more) working six hours a day (preferably more). The chemistry of playmaking – that is, the personality elements of all members of the cast interacting – is the essential catalyst that brings the thing to life. In the hour at my disposal today it is clearly impossible for me to deal with the other six characters in the play in any detail. Therefore I have elected, quite deliberately, for the selfish point of view. Lest you be in danger of misunderstanding my intention, I must stress that partisanship is the vital protective standpoint one takes in order to give one's character the dignity of selfhood. That is, each character must be in the right *for himself*. It is up to the director to balance out those strong selfhoods emanating from each character in order to give the play drive and vision. It is *he* who must sort out 'right' and 'wrong' – but the *actor* must never stand in moral judgment on his own character. Never. Enough said. I like Francis Bacon's (the painter, not the other one) description of art as being 'planned accident'. I shall now try to share with you as much of the planning and the accident as I can.

I had scribbled on the front of my script a fraction of a poem by Verlaine:

> *Et je m'en vais*
> *Au vent mauvais*
>   *Qui m'emporte*
> *Deçà, delà,*
> *Pareil à la*
>   *Feuille morte.*

'I go with the evil wind, carried here, carried there, as a dead leaf is.' It was Hedda's epitaph; and it went straight to my heart because I knew that the one thing I understood about Hedda, before even beginning to rehearse, was that she was a prey to *her* strong heart, pumping away inside her healthy body. I get no feeling of illness from her. Rather – too much life. But I knew she suffered from an ancient disease, the name of which we have almost lost in our times and in our language. *Accidie*. *Nadryv*. Rendering the world black. Making even the autumn leaves outside the window not melancholy, not autumnal, not exquisite, but withered. A prisoner of her heart? Impulsive then? Not an adjective easily ascribed to Hedda, but I knew that it was the one for me.

As I have mentioned, to act a character is to be entirely partisan about that character. You must defend that character to the death. You must love her as you love yourself. You must, if necessary, loathe her as you loathe yourself. So one thing only was clear. If Hedda was *merely a calculating animal* she was not interesting to me. If she was *simply unreasonably malevolent* she was an unworthy individual. What demon winds blew her about? What did she get hurt by? What defensive about? What did she love? What bored her? What excited her? When did she lie? When tell the truth? What made her laugh? What cry?

Now I have to explain that I had played Hedda before. That was some five years ago and it was for the television, and it was a pretty good production all in all. But the thing that is infuriating about that medium, with a difficult play like this one, is that no sooner do you get a glimpse of what other paths open up to you as you hasten round the maze of her character, than the game is over. The thing is recorded. Done. Finished. I came away from that knowing I had a long way to go. Certain mysteries remained mysteries to me. I had to clear them up – just for myself. And luckily I had the chance. It arose almost accidentally, this second production, and landed up having a healthy commercial run at the Duke of York's Theatre last year – *alors, à bas* those who grumble that Ibsen is box-office poison! But more importantly for me, it meant that I could explore this elusive creature at length, if not at leisure.

So now – to begin at the beginning. You start by understanding something about the character in a general sort of way. You feel a pull. You perceive a sort of powerful unhappiness. You think back. You recall, all too easily, the high points – just as everyone else does. The hat. The shot at the judge. The drink. Burning the manuscript.

Giving the gun. The final shot. But what about the bits in between? You begin to be consumed by a raging curiosity. *What made her do these things?* Why, why, why? And how, how, how? I bet if I were to ask any ordinary mortal what led up to these strange and haunting events, not *one* of them would be able to tell me with any exactitude whatsoever. 'How could she!' they cry. Or, 'How dreadful. I can't forgive her for that! She made him drink . . . she gave him a pistol . . . she burned his book. . . . Unpardonable! Evil!' 'Unfair!' I cry back. 'She's no Iago. There's a *reason*. These ravings won't do.' And with a sigh of relief, you loose your hold on objectivity and allow that blessed selfishness that I mentioned earlier to engulf you entirely. You're on Hedda's side at last.

Each one of us, thinking back on a bad moment in our lives, shudders at the memory; but deep down we know *why* it happened. Or like the car accident (unless you fell asleep at the wheel) there is *always* a version, full of detail and self-justification. Hedda *never* falls asleep at the wheel. But what exactly is the story she might choose to tell? It is my job to find out.

A writer must start a thesis or a re-examination of his subject with a full knowledge of what has been written about it before. I propose that it is vital that an actor should be innocent. Not ignorant – but innocent. You read a lot around the work if you feel the interest. Indeed, looking at photographs of the period can be especially useful. From them you glean more about furnishing, clothes, manners, demeanour, than from any sociological tract. Julia Margaret Cameron's portraits, for example, will tell you more about Victorian women and how they regarded themselves than many a novel. Perhaps you might even have seen a performance or two. That's daunting enough. Even more daunting is the knowledge that there are a few plays, a very few – and this is one of them – that seem to have passed into the realm of public property. *Hamlet* is another. Quite erroneously people imagine that they know the play intimately. It somehow belongs to them. They feel positively proprietorial about it. It's *their* play. But you cannot, must not, for your very life, allow these things to infect your instinct. Nothing on God's earth will help you except that great matter, and the text itself. So to the text you go – and to the devil with preconceptions.

Reading as I did the Norwegian original, I was struck, although I must admit that I don't speak the language, by its verve and simplicity. No long words. Banal everyday phrases. A proliferation of expletives like 'Good God!' No French in the conversations with

Brack. Just one or two words of Danish, I'm told, to denote sophistication or 'in-talk'. So, after all, small-town Hedda and small-town Brack were a bit less adept at witty small-talk than I had realised. Natural-sounding words. Idiosyncratic. Of course there were many difficulties, as there must be in any work in translation – like the famous one of where Eilert Løvborg shot himself. I remember consulting the good doctor Jonathan Miller about this problematic area and asking him (although we know quite well *where* Ibsen meant, in what one might perhaps call the lower living quarters) how we could find the best euphemism for *underlivet*. 'Ah, yes, yes,' he mused. 'Well, under the liver lies the hypochondria. No! No! Shot himself in the hypochondria doesn't quite do, does it?' Loin, thigh, bowel, lower stomach . . . Well, in the end it must be left to the actor concerned to find the word he can invest most sinisterly with the greatest clarity. And that in fact became our chiefest aim. To find the simplest, most meaningful, yet most reverberative word, all along the way. And nothing dated, or archaic, or too clever. Suffice it to say that our intentions were to try to get away from its sounding like a translation at all, if possible.

'Read my plays carefully', says Ibsen; and this injunction must be obeyed to the letter. The actor misses a trick at his peril. The play is constructed like a first-rate thriller. Ibsen scatters clues all along the way of it and you *must* find them. And you *must* help the audience find them. An audience for this play has to be very awake. Very attentive. They have to listen hard. It is not a play easy on the ears. Most of us do not listen hard, alas. Most of us are already starting to put together a reply before our interlocutor has closed his mouth. But in this play we discovered that every word that a character utters springs *directly* out of what another has just said. There are no apparent *non-sequiturs* as there are in, say, Chekhov. The only exceptions to this are the five references to vine-leaves made by Hedda. Those lines of hers are in secret code understood only by Løvborg. They are her own heated adolescent vision of him. I like to imagine that she must have come across a picture of a Greek statue (like the ravishing Bacchus in the Bargello) in a book in her father's library, an intriguing find amongst all those boring volumes of military history. Fig-leafed or no, it embodied for her an irresistible idea of this electric Bohemian visitor to her house. Forget theories about the Dionysiac world-view or *Zeitgeist* or whatever. All that is for the delectation of the scholars. Hedda is no scholar and she delights in a much more sensuous vision. It is a vision which fades with a perfect diminuendo between the end of Act II and the end of Act III. At that point, when there is a job to be done, reality takes over from the dream, and the years'-old secret ceases to thrill. It dies, and is discarded forever. Free death, not free life, takes its place in Hedda's hierarchy.

I must, because of time, skate swiftly over this vast initial area of work. My script of the play is as complete a working examination of *Hedda Gabler* as you are likely to find – communal work. There is not, I think, one second from curtain-up to curtain-down that is not 'mined', to use Ibsen's favourite word. There is even work that has to do with that foggy time before the play actually begins. I invented a complete honeymoon itinerary, by the way – all six ghasty months of it. (They had a dreadful fight in Bruges, in case you didn't know.) One important decision was to use Jørgen and not the usual 'George' – which seems as daft as calling Chekhov's Masha 'Mary'. This *naming of names* in the play was, of course, most particularly looked at: who is familiar with whom; the derisory – or affectionate – Auntie for Aunt; when is Løvborg called Eilert; the misnaming of Thea; Tesman's persistently forgetting Thea's married name; the required intimacy in Thea's being wooed into using Hedda's christian name; the threat in Brack's using it, and the equal threat in his using her married name; the mockery in his elevating her from quondam Miss Hedda, the daughter of his old chum the General, to Madame Hedda (she has by degrees dwindled into a wife!); when is Judge Brack reduced to plain Mr; Eilert's accolade in calling her simply Hedda Gabler; her rudeness in referring to Berta as 'the girl'; her refusing to be familiar with her husband's name, until she forgets in the heat of things; generals, professors, prime ministers, doctors – in short, all the bourgeois reverberations engendered by the title of the play itself. This pre-work covered, too, the house they had just moved into and its furnishing – courtesy of Brack; what new clothes she'd bought (the fight in Bruges, perhaps?); what had been unpacked the night before (Daddy's portrait was still to have a place found for it, I was certain); the flowers – Thea's little bunch lost among the glory of Brack's tributes; the aggressive dreariness of the old piano; and so on.

And what do you *do* – for Heaven's sake! – when you get up in the morning, in a house new to you, a servant you don't know or like, no father, no interests, no horse, no friends. I wondered a lot about Hedda's so-called popularity. I don't believe she had many friends really. She is the kind of creature who gives the *impression* of being *so* sought after, that in the end no one asks her out. I think the line: 'I suppose all our best friends are still in the country', is one of the most forlorn I have ever heard.

Despised domesticity . . . and despised motherhood. I have actually heard it said that Hedda's pregnancy is in dispute! How odd. But still, even G. B. S. in his résumé in *The Quintessence of Ibsenism* fails utterly to notice this most central condition. Male chauvinism run mad! Apart from Auntie's broad hints, there are at least a dozen references to it made by Hedda during the play, starting with, 'God yes, September already!' in Act I. Anyone who thinks this is a mere botanical reference to the state of the trees needs his head examined! It means, quite simply, that there are four months to go. And I can never forget, although Tesman does, that she kills *two* people at the end of the play. I found, in fact, that the pregnancy drew together every strand of the play so fundamentally that to doubt it for an instant would quite simply jeopardise the playing of it:

(i) Power over other people: she has none over her child. It will grow and grow. She cannot influence it. Cannot stop it. Hardly knows how it began.

(ii) Sexuality: her disappointment and bewilderment over what she *imagined* the act of love to be, and what it actually *was* are appalling. 'You haven't any idea about anything much', she snarls at Tesman. Poor fellow – what could he know?

(iii) Vanity: like a monster, it will make her grow ugly and fat.

(iv) Physicality: her loathing of being touched by people she finds unappetising. What an excuse her admitting to the baby would be for cloying affection from Auntie, for husbandly handling from Tesman, for despised clucking from Berta, for deferential mocking from the Judge!

(v) Freedom: the baby curtails even thinking about that possibility more powerfully than a prison could.

(vi) Life: it is a force that mocks her fascination with death at every turn.

(vii) Beauty: her ideas of the aesthetic and the romantic are in danger of being made absurd by the baby's existence. You lie back, close your eyes, and wallow in alluring and fearful dreams of Eilert. And it's not even his! It is a terrible thing to be carrying the child of the man you dislike while the image of the man you love is carried in your head. For *love*, read *obsession* if you prefer. It's all one. 'Nothing serious has happened you mean?' – Ha! The Judge should only know! 'But for God's sake it was only a book!' – No one can say her sense of proportion is impaired.

(viii) Self-definition: in this most territorially imperative of people, this unwanted thing has dared to invade her life. 'Careful, don't presume too far', she warns Eilert, because not even he must dare to explain her to herself. She means, surely, don't come too close . . . I must have air round me . . . don't tread on me . . . I flinch . . . I hurt . . . be careful of my soul . . . it's dangerous. 'I never jump', she says. Well, she's jumped – and it's unbearable.

I believe that she cannot equate living with compromise, and in that sense is more true to herself than anyone else in the play. Tesman will adapt. Berta will adapt. Auntie will adapt. The Judge will adapt. Thea will do anything to adapt. Eilert tried and failed. Hedda cannot try and must not fail. Paralysed by her own perfectionism, tied down by the lack of alternatives, devoured by the unquestioning greedy lives around her and inside her, where is she to direct that nervous animal energy of hers? She must be central to everyone's attention and not peripheral. She must know everything and commit herself to nothing. The baby forbids that. And what a commitment to the future it is! Her final act is a combination of expertise and taste. But it is also an absolute necessity, and in that sense it is an act of passion and commitment.

Up to now I have touched on Hedda's inner being – only touched on it – in order to bring you with me to the point at which I began. I said that if she were *merely* a calculating animal I could not justify her. I want you to be as partisan as I am. I want you to know what it is like to be Hedda, to look through her retina, to feel what pressures are upon her, to understand what she does at any given point – and then to see *why* she does what she does at that second. I can't make you *feel* those things – that is the prerogative of performance – but maybe I can lead you to see the deep-down selfishness of the human animal in a corner.

Acting is a process of diminishing your choices. And then making those choices inevitable. That and only that is what the creature *must* do or say at that second. If a sort of encephalographic computer were attached to the brain lobes during a performance, the possible choices at each given moment would be myriad. I can perhaps make you aware of the choices open to me, but the *final* one I make must appear incontrovertible. Edith Evans once said something like this: that if a bolt of lightning were to strike her at any point during a play, the resulting statue would look right for eternity. The moment, in other words, would be truthful. That, at any rate, is what we lesser mortals strive for.

Now I suggest that Hedda, true to her nature, and true to her words ('Sometimes something comes over me. Just like that. I can't explain it') says and does things throughout the play which she *cannot forsee the result of*. She lives very dangerously in fact. She takes terrific chances. And most often she faces the consequences with an almost disarming candour. These strange and dreadful things happen because she is *ready* for them. She is spoiling for something when she gets up in the morning, and by the next midnight she is dead.

Do you know anyone who would take revenge on an intrusive aunt-in-law by pretending to mistake her hat for the maid's, driven to mischief by Tesman's horrid childhood slippers? And then she has the gall, not once but twice, to ask if Auntie might have been offended by the 'business'; *and* the gall to admit to Brack that she had done it on purpose. She didn't plan the incident. Didn't *know* she was going to say it until she says it. The fury was there . . . the hat was there . . . the Aunt was there . . . Bingo!

Do you know anyone who would threaten to shoot at someone with a real live bullet in a primed gun, and then *actually shoot*? She was sure of her aim, I must admit – one of her few accomplishments, and it served her well. But did she apologise? No. She did not.

Do you know anyone who would entertain the monstrous idea of burning someone's hair off, and then actually light a taper and go to do it? Simply for the hell of it. (How gratifying to see Thea so terrified, and how lucky for her that Berta interrupts!) Well, that's what I did. It seemed so consistent with her nature. She dares all the time. It was a word that hammered like a *leitmotif* through the play. Ibsen uses that simple word 'dare' again and again and again.

Do you know anyone who would help a person to kill himself by actually handing him the means to do it? It seems perfectly logical. If he wants to, he must be helped. It's his decision. She doesn't apologise for that either.

Do you know anyone who would take a singular and original piece of writing and throw it in a fire? And then later admit to that crime as wide-eyed as a bad child.

Do you know anyone who would react to the death of a lover with undisguised elation? And then explain why without shame. Her so-called social conventionality is of a *very* unsentimental kind it seems!

Do you know anyone who would admit to being an accessory to a suicide, and then despise the man who would cover up that fact, as being dishonourable?

I can only conclude that this extraordinary person is a liar. If she is not, then what on earth is she doing? Testing . . . testing . . . one . . . two . . . three . . . four . . . am I alive? . . . am I in love? . . . am I powerful? . . . how much will people take of me? . . . how much can I take of myself? . . . do I merit the gift of life, and if life is not a gift should I bother with it? The other people are the antidote to her own vibrancy, except for one. That one is Eilert. The others hem her in, disgust her, bore her, annoy her, desolate her. They are the prose to Eilert's poetry. And to poetry – compressions, metaphors, mysteries – she responds.

Before getting to him, bear with me a while longer about Hedda's desperation, her loneliness, otherwise the triad of her 'crimes' might seem a touch heartless, not to say arbitrary. I'm talking, of course, of the drink, the gun, and the burning. So let's just see where she *openly* reveals herself. She does it covertly all the time, but let's look at the overt declarations.

The first is where she is left alone, and wordless, in Act 1. It amounts to what I would call a silent soliloquy. Ibsen has a stage direction, but there is no need to follow it slavishly as long as his intention – that of showing a restless unhappy creature – is respected. I saw the slippers on the carpet as I roamed around the cage of this room, and it seemed the only thing to do was to kick them out of the way, hateful things. I saw the portrait of my father. and flew to it as if to draw comfort from the man who had left me in this mess; and then I felt foolish as the lifeless old boy stared back at me. I felt claustrophobia and nausea closing me in and rushed to fling aside the curtains I perversely had closed, and to lean there gulping in the fresh air. At this point, when Tesman comes back into the room, if she were a single-minded, uncomplex, liberated sort of individual, she would certainly have grounds enough to turn back into the room and say to her husband: 'Look, I hate this house, I hate your family, your work bores me, you bore me, we've had six hellish months together, I think I see that this marriage is never going to work – so I'm going to leave you. Goodbye.' But the woman can't do that. She's pregnant, has no money of her own, no old family house to go back to; they live in a small town where the gossip would be intolerable – her father's name would be smirched; she's too proud to walk the streets and *needs* the safety of a bourgeois household to enclose her fragile self-respect. These things are

obvious. And this is Hedda Gabler we are talking about. Society
doesn't like mavericks, and we shall have to see whether society
wins. Tesman tries to pull her into that society by offering: 'You're
one of the family now.' And she?: 'I don't know about that.' She is
fighting the comfortable communality of marriage from the start –
because it means nothing to her. She has bought her 'annuity' and
even *that* is diminishing by the end of the act. She has 'made her
bed', but is having a devilish time lying in it.

There is another silent soliloquy at the beginning of Act II. Ibsen
describes in the stage directions merely Hedda's readiness to receive
visitors, and that she is busy loading the gun. So – the furniture is
now moved round to the dispositions she prefers. Father's picture is
by now in its place of honour on the wall of the inner room. Her old
piano is likewise in that sanctum. The flowers are less profuse and
more carefully placed. (She doesn't, by the way, dislike flowers as I
have heard someone unhelpfully declare; she dislikes *Brack's*
flowers. Now if Eilert had sent them . . . just think!) The house is
quiet. Tesman has gone out. Berta probably has her poor old
exhausted feet up. Hedda has changed into an afternoon dress. A
dull day. What will happen?

I thought perhaps I might not load the gun in full view. Gives the
game away too soon. (I say game advisedly: Brack knows her
predilections of old.) If you are loading a gun it is pretty obvious
that you will be using it sooner or later. And what about the piano?
Why not play it? But she's too unsettled to sit down. So, I ran the
butt of the gun down the keys. An ugly sound. Defiant. I wandered
into the main room surveying the newly arranged furniture. It was
better than it had been, but neither pleased me nor displeased me. I
shoved the back of the rocking-chair as I passed. It rocked noisily on
its own. Ghostly. I stood, unsure of what to do, toying with time.
Time toying with me? The clock ticked. I remembered the gun in
my hand and began polishing it with a piece of lint. What a splendid
gleaming weapon. I loved it. I checked the sights and turned to take
mock-aim at something. Daddy's frozen glare caught my eye. I
hated him. I nearly squeezed the trigger. Patricide! Don't bother
you fool – he's well and truly dead. Ah, but what does it feel like to
kill *yourself*, I thought. I slowly brought the gun to my own temple,
interested by the feel of cold metal on warm skin. It felt good to me,
and strangely desirable. I must investigate whether this looks as
ferocious and beautiful as I think. I went to the mirror above the
desk to look, and posed in front of it – as an actress might, I fancied.

A stray wisp of hair annoyed me. Spoiled the picture. I smoothed it into place, diverted from morbidity by vanity. I wished fleetingly I had hair like Thea's. I heard the crackle of leaves from outside, and whirled round to see the figure of the Judge picking his way towards my house. The back way! How dare he, I thought. Too presumptuous by half. I shall give him a fright. So I did!

Now I expect the purist will tut. But I don't mind. For me this one minute charade expanded her dilemma most explicitly. Emptiness, boredom, pistols, vanity, death and dying, time creeping past. 'Well, for God's sake, what am I to do?' she cries to the Judge. What indeed?

The ensuing scenes with Brack are astonishingly frank. She answers everything he asks with truthfulness. He pretends to be shocked here and there, but I don't believe he really is. Intrigued, yes. She is what the French call an *allumeuse*. And how odd her behaviour is to him. But secretly he is delighted that the way is opening up for him.

Why is she so disloyal to Tesman? The mischief titillates her, certainly. But I also think she cannot bear the effort of pretending to connubial bliss another moment. As I have said, she is spoiling for something, and having correctly gauged the extent of Brack's hypocrisy, can trust him with her own. (When she refers to 'our sort of person', does she mean their common gentility or corruption?) She is, in addition, searching for some reassurances from him, that she might not have made as big a mistake in marrying Tesman as she fears. A dark cloud settles on Hedda, for a moment here, a moment there, incomprehensible to Brack; but it lifts again: 'My time was up. Oh, no, I mustn't say that, or even think it', and 'this place smells of death'. How can he understand that she is half in love with the easeful thing? She is hiding precious little when she says things like: 'I have made my bed, I shall have to . . . I was about to say' (a realist struggling to get out); 'No obligations for me' (the realist is losing the unequal struggle); 'Boring myself to death' (the realist again). I had thought, during the first few weeks of the play's run, that her *sotto voce* comment to Tesman's generous and envious, 'I could never write anything like this' (referring to Eilert's new book) was simply cutting and funny. But gradually I discovered that her unadorned, 'Hm . . . No. No' spoke worlds of sorrow and disappointment as she watched her two writers.

Her self-dislike is overwhelming: 'Courage. Yes. Well that is the thing to have. Then one can survive anything.' She is talking about herself, and crying with anger inside at what she knows she lacks. (And *at the very same moment* she's turning, swift as a lioness, on Eilert – as if to say, 'Well now, let's see if *you* have this vaunted thing.' But we will come back to that anon). 'If only you could understand how poor I am, and you have the chance to be so rich', she says to Thea. And if ever Hedda weeps openly at her own 'halfness' it is here. I don't know of another place where she despises her own nature more vulnerably or more completely. (Unless it be in Act IV with, 'Why does everything I touch become ludicrous and ugly?') But after this helpless breakdown, eliciting unwanted pity from Thea, she must recover herself with some familiar wickedness, with playing a game. Hedda's games tend to turn frighteningly serious before you can say knife (or pistol). Undoubtedly, she can charm people easily enough when she bothers to. But can she affect their *lives*? Can she change the course of her own? Shall she not have a go at frightening Thea as much as she is frightened by herself?

I'm still looking at the chinks in Hedda's armour where the light is let in for an instant, so we can trace the compulsions in her nature that drive her to do what she does. Act III now. Tesman says: 'I'm going to confess something to you, Hedda. When he'd finished reading, an ugly feeling came over me.' Ugly? But that's *my* prerogative, she's thinking. I am full of ugly feelings, but I have to live with them. But you? You have them too? Good God! The play is full of little repetitions like that, and there is this golden rule: when things are repeated, they are repeated out of shock or surprise. Perhaps Agatha Christie might use the device for emphasis, but not Ibsen.

The line, as Hedda asks Tesman about the manuscript she'll later destroy – 'But surely this could be rewritten, couldn't it?' – went through dozens of variations. It seems such a clueless question. Was it rhetorical, since she must have known it couldn't? Was she playing the innocent child to conform with Tesman's paternalism? ('This is man's work, my dear, don't you trouble your pretty little head about it', he sometimes seems to imply.) Was it said to enrage him, by belittling the work of scholars? Or maybe she *really* doesn't understand the importance of the original, and is asking a genuine question. Certainly Hedda is not much interested in books. Well, acting being the chemical thing it is – everyone on stage affecting you in some way – the manner in which I asked the question usually depended on how much Tesman was hungover, how much he was irritating me. The importance of it is that his *reply* makes the manuscript infinitely more precious and powerful an object to her than it was before.

Tesman asks her to come with him to his dying aunt. 'No. No. Don't ask me to do that. I don't want to know about illness or death. I can't stand ugly things.' Straight from the heart. I think she feels tearful with horror. I don't think it's a line lightly said, or a sophisticated fobbing-off of Tesman. She means it! The fact of death is untenable to her. It's too attractive. And then, too, her own fascination with it at this stage: Gothic, glamorous, Romantic. To die peacefully in bed, of old age, with your loved ones round you, is not a vision that she can contain in her view of things. It implies a long and comfortable life, for one thing, and hers so far has been short and troubled. No great falls from glory? No marks left on the world? A serene demise ending a serene existence? No! To expend all this pain on surviving from day to petty day, and then to be denied a grand exit, would render each day even more meaningless than is bearable.

Another impulsive gesture, for the plot probably the most crucial of all, happens at the end of this scene. The manuscript, precious as the Holy Grail to her now, is in Tesman's hands. He's on the point of leaving for a nap and then to read it and return it to its owner. She remembers the letter, summoning Tesman to the dying aunt, almost negligently. Tesman puts the manuscript down to read it. She can't take her eyes off it. It seems to be radiating power like a piece of plutonium. He becomes distracted with concern for his dying aunt and pleads with her to come with him. She refuses *con passione*, exhorts him impatiently to 'run'. The Judge is announced. The domestic flapdoodle is at its height. Poor old Berta in a tizzy. Hedda is dying to hear the Judge's gossip and agrees to see him, callously forgetful of Tesman's worries. Tesman overlooks the manuscript on his way out. She reminds him of it since it's so important to him. He wheels back for it, pulling on his gloves the while. She, suddenly covetous, hugs it to her, and says no, she'll hang on to it for him. That seems acceptable to the trusting fellow, and off he muddles, bumping into the Judge, and this diversion allows her to whip it under the sofa-cushions. God knows why. Some instinct says hide it from the Judge. And there it is – burning a hole in the cushions. The Judge stretches out on the sofa, impudent monster. Hedda has a secret, though what's to be done with it she has no idea. She enjoys the intrigue mightily. For a bit.

She's deeper in blood now – they all are. It's a dangerous game.

'Little fool, meddling with a man's life.' Little Thea, all good intentions and solicitude, is blurring the hard edges of Eilert, forcing him to be what he's not. It's like being loved by a marshmallow! Hedda sees the immorality of emotional bribery. To be free, albeit dissolute, is one thing. To be bound by hoops of honey is another. That free-will Hedda sets such store by is eroded by a curly-headed mouse. Eilert is Hedda's peer and she does not like him being tampered with. She sees how dangerous it is to toy with a man's better nature. She is scared of the outcome.

At the beginning of Act IV Ibsen again writes his own scenario. I obeyed it pretty well. Perhaps I ought in all honesty to add an aside here, which is that all stage directions are a drag. If they are good ones, they describe to you the author's intentions as regards the characters' inner state. If they are bad, they dictate to you and should be disregarded. Acting styles change drastically. What might have been a fine gesture for Janet Achurch is not especially fine for Janet Suzman. So – I obeyed Ibsen but added a cigarette, which made her retch. (She hadn't refused Tesman's offer of a cigarette in Act II for nothing.) It's physiologically unpleasant to smoke when you are pregnant. And I couldn't bear to be near the stove. Think what had recently happened there. Fresh air again. I had to have it. She's waiting. Waiting. Has he done it? Is it over?

Auntie comes in. Oh, God, social niceties. She makes the effort. But the cosily smug description of how old Aunt Rina died sends Hedda's mind recoiling back to her own satanic script, from where it peers darkly out from time to time. 'Oh, thoughts. You can't control them', she says. (Remember, 'Oh reason, reason', in Act II.) The door swings open to Hedda's soul again. It's a turmoil in there. Then there's another revealing line that always meant a lot to me: 'You'll be lonely now, Miss Tesman.' She understands loneliness. For a second she allows herself to sympathise with the old lady. To be young and lonely is horrible enough. To be old and lonely? No! They just *might* have become friendlier here; but Auntie, true to form, smothers her with baby promises again. The fragile chance is lost.

'It's killing me, all this. It's killing me.' In our production we went very far in this scene where Hedda confesses she's pregnant. We had found that the characters in the play, far from conforming to our English notion of Scandinavian gloom and self-control (*pace* Ingmar Bergman), were as ebullient, noisy, emotional, shockable, excitable, tearful and nervous as the next man. Certainly, in the three scenes where Hedda and Tesman are by themselves, with no stranger present, a certain public mask dropped from both of us. Well, to be brief: Tesman became so enraged to hear what Hedda had done with the manuscript that he began to strike her very violently. She was so shocked and frightened at his anger that her initial desperate lie was as self-protective as it was mendacious. But when he, all innocence and flattered affection, says, 'I never realized you loved me so much', she has no choice – sickened by his trusting nature and sickened by her own deceit – but to attempt to tell him the truth about the baby. The ensuing noisy joy is too much to bear for the woman killed by kindness. For it *is* killing her. The residue of this (to her) humiliating and horrible happening, certainly bleeds into her cry later on of how she's cursed when everything she touches 'becomes ludicrous and ugly'. For her life *is* ludicrous. Eilert's death is ludicrous. They have that still in common. And how perfect that Tesman and Thea, made for each other from the start, will put their blond heads together till Kingdom Come in order to sort out the writings of a man they will never understand. The absurdity is sublime. Hedda laughs. I mean *really* laughs. As Garbo laughed.

I have in my possession a most treasured thing. It is a creased, torn, mucky, paperback script of this play that belonged to Mrs Patrick Campbell. It was given to me by Peggy Ashcroft, who was given it by John Gielgud. I am in awe of it and the hands it has passed through. But when I look at it, I have hardly any clues to the magic that was drawn out of the pages by Mrs Pat. Only the reiterated scrawl in large writing, in pencil, of the word 'laughs'. She's right, naturally enough. Hedda laughs a lot . . . self-mocking, mocking others, sometimes genuinely amused, sometimes bleakly amused at her own awful predicament. She has no mean sense of humour. But here in the venerable old script, where I had somehow expected to find the big laugh, is a puzzlingly clean page. At 'You Jørgen, your life!' – a blank. The blankest page in the whole dog-eared wonder. Where I had scrawled 'laughs' in mine, she had left no clue. For a woman who reputedly had the wickedest tongue on the English stage, the omission is unexpected. But on second thoughts, it is also a heartening confirmation of how elastic the part is. If we had coincidentally reached the same conclusion, Mrs Pat and I, the infrastructure of the play would be demonstrably less complex than it is. I'm glad we didn't.

And so onwards to the last lap of Hedda's self-revelations. Her disgust with the Judge is a complete feeling. Good clean despisal. He has trod on her heart, come in the 'back way' once too often. She has cried out in pain: 'Not free. Still not free! No! I can't bear that thought. Never!' It's true, she's not free, and Eilert is not free, roaming disfigured and shamed, bereft of vine-leaves, in Pluto's shade. The way is clear.

Ibsen has a stage direction that, of all of them, I liked best. 'People resign themselves to that sooner or later', coos the Judge – and *she returns his gaze*. It's good, that one. Clear and meaningful. And she says: 'Perhaps they do.' Perhaps *they* do – but I'm not 'people'.

Now, light and amused, she touches objects for the last time. The clock. The two fair heads. Plays with Tesman's pipe. Like Cleopatra, she fights for life to the very last moment: 'Can't I help you two at all?' I sometimes wondered what might have happened if Tesman had replied roundly, 'Yes, you can.' But he can't even see what's happening in front of his very nose. The moment is irretrievable. And straightway something like this invades her being: 'With one long breath, caught and held in his chest, he fought his sadness over his solitary life. Don't cry, you idiot! Live or die, but don't poison everything . . .' (I was in need of a poet to help me describe the shadowy thing lurking beneath the dangerous surface-calm, and I found one. What more anguished and delicate insight than that? It is by Saul Bellow, from his novel *Herzog*.) Courage . . . courage . . . and the world well lost.

At long last I can get to the centre of the play. Eilert Løvborg occupies most of it, and certainly most of Hedda's thoughts. I shall examine the three most haunting events from *Hedda's point of view*.

(i) *Tempting him to drink.* Never forget that when Eilert Løvborg enters the room for the first time, Hedda stays silent for nigh on five minutes. Is that a woman totally in command of herself? I think her knees have gone wobbly. I think her heart is racing for the first time in five years. And how has he changed? (One day I'd like to see an Eilert who has really gone to seed, what with all Thea's wholesome cooking!) Matching up a dream to a reality is a hard thing to do. And then, comparing her husband to her 'lover', the one ignorant of the past, the other all too aware of it. And so on. Then dredging up poignant memories over the photograph album . . .

What exactly did happen on that long ago day when she threatened to shoot him? I know what Ibsen *said* he meant, but the subtext is downright impenetrable. The actual happening is inaccessible unless you read Ibsen's notes, and the audience cannot do that. Certainly what occurred must have been extreme. At the risk of sounding simplistic, imagine this scene: their sides must have touched as they sat whispering together on the sofa, pretending to pore over a magazine while Daddy snored away. An unaccountable excitement at Eilert's proximity must have suffused Hedda. It must have confused and scared her. His 'confessions' must have appalled and intrigued her. To a girl bewildered by her own intemperate physicality, the reaction to a pass from Eilert must have been out of all proportion. So, for the purposes of the play, this will do: one evening Eilert tried to rape her. (A mere grab would have seemed like rape to her.) She was terrified and grabbed a gun. He fled. She never forgave him for fleeing! (Was she aware of a certain cowardice in him, corresponding to hers? Yet another link in the chain of comradeship.) Note that he disdains a reply to her accusation, 'How could you abuse your good friend like that?' *Why* does he evade her, upset as she is by memory? Is it the silence of guilt? Is it the silence of cowardice? Is it the silence of acquiescence to which there is no defense? He replies instead with a death-wish. (And there's *another* link between them.) Not a happy man, then. What on earth has happened to him? What has Thea done to unman him so?

Hedda then admits, in my opinion, to a blatantly physical passion for Eilert. Again, the text is tantalisingly ambiguous, even obscure. I'm referring to the line: 'That was not my worst act of cowardice that evening.' Certainly the innuendo is clear enough to Eilert. Talking, as they must, in euphemisms, he understands at last what it was she wanted – *and* what he missed. But she, vulnerable again, stops any further intrusion on her inmost feelings. She will *not* be defined, even by him. And if there is regret in her heart, she is too proud to show it.

Thea comes in, and they seem to have secrets which Hedda has not shared. She is jealous. So, her pet demon is wearing an apron! Her wild animal has been domesticated! She has got to rock the boat. She cannot bear this friendly intimacy between them, this smug ownership of her Eilert. She must be 'in the middle'.

Eilert, thrown by Hedda, then precipitates his own downfall. I can't help thinking of Breughel's 'The Fall of Icarus'. The great event seems hardly to be happening. With each phrase, another feather falls from his wings: 'Isn't she lovely?' 'We're good close comrades.' (Remember, that was his endearment to Hedda – and she still smarts from discovering he also uses it with Thea.) 'We trust each other completely.' 'She has the courage to follow her beliefs.' (Even if *you* don't, my beauty, he implies.) Hedda, slighted and much hurt, turns swiftly to the one thing she knows might hurt him back. 'Let's see if you have the courage to follow *your* principles, then', she warns him inwardly, and leaps into offering him a drink. He stands firm. Her blood is up. She tries another tack, by trying to charm him. He is maddeningly impervious. Nothing can stop her now. She resorts to testing this vaunted trust between them. He angers, and takes the bait. She despises him for it immediately. '*Me* wanted it? Are you mad?' she replies to Thea. And it's only the truth. She offered him what he really wanted, and he took it – the more fool he. It was all too easy, and she dislikes Thea even more for softening him up so.

She has to stop him drinking too much, though. The whole thing is getting out of hand, which is *not* what she bargained for. He must go to the party if he wants to go on drinking. A free man. And then she can picture him with vine-leaves in his hair – Bacchus restored. Far rather that than the sight of him here – wine dribbling out of his mouth, shaking with weak anger. The dream is always more attractive than the reality. What I am suggesting in describing this scene is that if Eilert Løvborg had not turned the knife himself, Hedda might not have thought of revenge. He baited her. She baited him. Passions make you cruel.

(ii) *Her offering him the pistol* should now present no problems. I hope I have by now shown how logical a thing it is for this Hedda of ours to do. The fact that it is also poetical, justly or no, is a tribute to the immensely powerful inner life of the two of them. Let me just add that they seem to have, both of them, a strong mutual understanding about death. They are two souls somehow at home with each other. They are, after all, the only two people who doubt the value of their own lives. Note again that Løvborg, unsolicited, suggests his own suicide. By now, her vision of him with vine-leaves in his hair is spent and faded. She can no longer 'live by thinking'. She has grown up. Death seems the most honourable and most desirable act to her. He must do it properly though – 'for once' in her life, his life. She's pleading – urgent – dreadfully intimate.

He starts to go. And *quite suddenly* she remembers how to help him. 'Wait!' She will divide her precious pistols. There's no one else she would allow to use them. The extent of their understanding is clear to see. He is not shocked by her gift. He simply reminds her of their old fantasies (the 'vine-leaves' code). He accepts the pistol with a simple 'thank you'. Regrets that she didn't save him the trouble before (the death-wish). No melodrama. No sentimentality. She is restored in his eyes to the old Hedda. She calls him seriously by his full name. He responds gravely with hers. Gravely enough for her to believe that he will do it – otherwise she would be unable to rise to the next act she must perform:

(iii) *The burning*. And now, left alone, trembling with the hope that he will end his life meaningfully, she has one great last thing to do for him. She must complete the parable of the lost child. She must cauterise Eilert out of her heart for ever.

Short of driving out to the nearest fjord and acting out Eilert's strange invention to the letter, the quickest way of rendering his lie truthful is the fire. The only way to cleanse *her* life of him, *his* life of Thea, and *both* of theirs of any despicable posthumous judgment, is to burn the book. The one way to revenge herself on meddling, stupid, childless, golden-haired Thea, is to burn the book. Thea will survive. Hedda has had moments of pity for her, but in the end her instinct is that Thea will adapt and survive. But for Eilert – far better a beautiful death than life with an unworthy *petite bourgeoise*. And for God's sake, it's only a book! All this drivel about its being a child is a ridiculous indulgence to a woman heavy with the real thing. Although I think she has some deeply painful awareness of both of them – the book and the child – being products of ill-matched unions.

Is there some doubt in Hedda's mind about the value of the work? After all, unpublished it is a conundrum. Published it would be assessable. I frankly don't believe Eilert when he boasts in Act II about its being his major work: 'My voice in every line.' Writers don't talk like that. Compare Trigorin in *The Seagull* – there speaks a true writer, it seems to me. There is also the hint of a possibility that it is a relief to him that it is gone. He certainly uses its loss to get rid of Thea, and he is implacable about doing so. He finally comes clean about the years 'up there': "I don't want to live her kind of life any more.' No wonder Hedda doesn't confess to having the manuscript! If she did, Thea would have to come back to him, and Eilert would be swamped all over again.

I had been holding the keys to the desk all the way through the scene between Thea and Eilert; and on the line, 'There's no future for her and me', I felt relief and triumph – even glee, perhaps – and I quietly lobbed the keys onto the desk top. My vacillation about whether to tell him or not that the book was safe and sound was over at last. Now, when he had left I found those keys, opened the drawer and took out the manuscript. (I had removed it from the sofa after Brack's exit, wondering what to do with the thing – but, scared of being found with it when I heard Eilert's voice raised in the hall, I locked it away.) I listened for sounds in the house. The floor creaked slightly as I moved. And I moved – irrevocably – towards the hot door of the stove. It burned my fingers as I opened it. The light and heat glared out at my eyes.

I knew it was terrible in one sense – but what Brack's 'people' might say was not a consideration to her. (Forgive me for veering between the first and third person.) I was impelled to do it. I *had* to clear the way for his death. I *had* to erase the past for him. It had to be as though Mrs Elvsted had never been.

Sometimes I would squat down, cradling and rocking the manuscript to me like a baby, gazing at the awful red coals. Sometimes I would just stand there, holding it lightly, not wanting to think of its important weight. I was waiting, though, for a surge of courage, and when it came I took it at the flood and threw the whole thing in. No delectating it, page by torn page. (I had done that in my previous version, but this Hedda seemed not to be able to savour the burning in the same way. She was less light-headed, more driven by those demon winds.) So I threw it in. Almost hurled it away from me. The flame caught. The edges curled. It smoked and flared up. It hurt my eyeballs. I slammed the door shut. Eilert was burning out of my system along with his burning book. I felt exhilarated and incredulous – but I had done it! My one act of total destruction was my one act of total liberation. Now it was up to him. He was free. Now he must free me. Only then did the words come. While revenging myself on Thea, I remember feeling jealousy and anguish, triumph and also pain. Unable to abort her own, she aborts Thea's 'child'. Hedda is trying to make some sort of sense out of a complex, symbolic, but above all impulsive act. She had done it first, articulated it afterwards.

The burning of the manuscript is so powerful a theatrical happening, that Act IV very often suffers from not being taken full cognisance of, as it should. The burning stays on in people's minds, but in Hedda's it is very quickly replaced by a far clearer flame. Act IV is most miraculously written and constructed. Not a word is out of place. Not a feeling muffed. Hedda travels at first a murky and thorny trail, but when at last she bursts out into the open and spies the lie of the land, she sees her own salvation gleaming darkly. She hugs to herself the greatest power she has ever experienced, that of escape and liberty, conquers her 'halfness', takes her innocent babe with her, and cocks a mighty snook at all the provincial paraphernalia of which she was fancied the very mark and glass.

She *cannot* be Auntie's child-bride, *cannot* be Thea's confidante, *cannot* be Berta's remote haus-frau, *cannot* be Tesman's supportive spouse, *cannot* be Brack's *maîtresse lointaine*. But, by God, she will be herself! Eilert's death, done with dignity, would have been a beacon to her. But he has only shown her how *not* to do it. Now she knows she has to take the whole burden on her own shoulders. They feel strangely less bowed as she does so. A dread lightness comes upon her. Jokes come easily. She arranges her scenario with such a sure touch that I fear, had she lived, another profession might have opened up to her in a more equal world!

The only utter mystery, akin to real life, resides in that moment which no one sees and no one can tell about – when she squeezes the trigger. But stop! Why should one want to? After all, it is only a play . . .

7 Ibsen's use of Language in *When We Dead Awaken*

JOHN NORTHAM

I could not think of a better play to base this paper on than Ibsen's last – for a variety of reasons. One is that, as a self-proclaimed Epilogue to his earlier work (however defined), it stands as in some sense an epitome of his art, and as such lends itself to a celebration of this 150th anniversary of his birth. Another is that I have recently felt a personal need to return to a play which has always disturbed rather than delighted me. I cannot claim to have emerged from the re-encounter with any momentous new insight; certainly I cannot emulate the brilliance of Professor McFarlane's recent Introduction to the last volume of his Oxford translations. I shall be restricting myself to a much more limited consideration of the language of the play and its structure to see how far these, in conjunction, might lead us to the 'meaning'.

As an Epilogue the play has already had its affinities with and echoes from earlier works exhaustively commented on. One of these, perhaps the most frequently noticed, has been the triangular relationship involving a man with two women who offer contrasted life-styles – a relationship that figures in Ibsen's very first play. And, it has been argued, it is manifestly active in his last; Rubek in his involvement with both Maja and Irene embodies the theme of the play, the inevitable antagonism between idealism in art and fulfilment in living. I want to begin by questioning that interpretation of the structure.

In what sense, after all, can we think of Rubek as being significantly *involved* with Maja, subject to any kind of temptation or attraction in her direction? In no sense. Rubek is mentally divorced, from the first scene or earlier. Emotionally estranged, he is not even held by those ties of obligation, duty, guilt that held Allmers, say, or

Solness or Rosmer. Maja means nothing to him.

Let me state, with deliberate baldness, an alternative reading of the structure. Ibsen offers us not a triangle but a square or parallelogram. Two of the characters, Rubek and Maja, are represented as individual human beings – representative beyond doubt, but fundamentally 'real'. Irene and Ulfheim, by contrast, exist less as 'real' characters than as representations of certain contrasted values, each offering temptation and exhortation to follow him or her to the making of a crucial, irreversible, life-determining choice. In my stark terms, figures closer to allegory than to 'real' life. The play as a whole I take to be a version of the morality play, with Irene and Ulfheim as 'virtue' and 'vice' acting upon two specimens of Everyman.

I shall soon be abandoning this highly simplified approach to the play, but before I do so, let me quickly substantiate it by what seems to me a monumentally simple set of direct comparisons and contrasts embedded in the structure and supported by the language.

The unity of action, though it involves two pairs of characters, is sustained in part by the physical and symbolic unity of the settings. Both pairs move together from sea-level to the heights until they reach the same point at which the crucial decision must be made. Each 'allegorical' figure bases his or her exhortation on the same verbal image of going up into the high mountains; and each is enveloped in potential irony in that the imagery is derived from the same source, St Matthew's gospel narrating Christ's temptation by the devil.

Irene's quotations from and references to St Matthew are frequent and, from the start, clearly attributable; Ulfheim's less so. In Act I, his invitation to Maja to sample the delights of mountain life reads like, and is, an example of bluff sexual opportunism.

ULFHEIM: I am making for high up in the mountains. – I don't suppose you've ever been in the high mountains, Mrs. Rubek? . . . Then you damn well see you get yourself up there this summer! You can come along with me. Both you and the professor . . . Come up into the mountains with me instead . . .

There, in the excellent Oxford translation, speaks the opportunist. But in the Norwegian we find a little verbal touch that makes Ulfheim's bluffness a veiled, half-muted reference to St Matthew.

ULFHEIM: *Helt opp på høyfjellet vil jeg.—De har vel aldri vært på høyfjellet, De frue?* ...
Død og pine, så se å komme Dem der opp nu i sommer da! De kan få følge med meg. Gjerne både De og professoren.

The similarity of action (tempting up into a high place) is blurred by an inexactness of language. The devil takes Jesus '*opp på et store höit Berg*' rather than '*opp på høyfjellet*'. But there is a word which, I believe, inclines us to sense the biblical behind the colloquial: the word '*følge*', 'follow'. 'You can come along with me' represents it perfectly in its modern currency; but it is also the word that is used again and again in the New Testament by and of Jesus: 'Jesus saith, follow me'; 'take up his cross, follow me'; 'sell that thou hast, follow me'; 'if any serve me, let him follow me', and so on. The biblical colouring encourages us to respond to the veiled biblical implications of Ulfheim's invitation.

In Act III, however, Ulfheim's equation with Irene as in some sense a 'tempter' is made exact by a very precise use of St Matthew's words, when he describes his involvement with a girl he once rescued from the gutter. The Oxford Ibsen again:

ULFHEIM: With these hands I carried her. I wanted to carry her through life like that . . . so that she shouldn't ever again bruise her foot against a stone!

It reads like a testament to personal experience; but it is the New Testament too. In the Norwegian the two texts are almost identical in essentials.

ULFHEIM: *På hendene bar jeg henne. Ville bære henne slik gjennem hele livet*; *på det at hun ikke skulle støte sin fot på noen sten.*

ST MATTHEW: *Han skal give sine Engle Befaling om dig, og* de skulle bære dig paa Hændene, *at du ikke skal støde din Fod paa nogen* Steen. (. . . *and in their hands shall they bear thee up, lest at any time thou dash thy foot against a stone.*)

Thus, as we approach the moment of choice, Ulfheim emerges clearly in a role parallel to Irene's. But of course the similarity serves to bring out the stark contrasts. Irene persists, to the end, in her endeavours to reach the heights and achieve, with Rubek, all the glory of the world; Ulfheim settles for the valley. Irene seeks spiritual marriage with Rubek; Ulfheim wants a love affair of sorts with Maja. Irene is a walking statue; Ulfheim a human wild animal. The process and the language of temptation are the same, but the two 'allegorical' figures represent opposed principles.

Even if you accept the figure of a parallelogram in place of a triangle, it may still be difficult to see these opposed principles in any new way; they still, as in the earlier figure, seem substantially to represent art versus life. Yet surely, in the last moments of the last Act, Ibsen produces one of those astounding reversals that reveal, almost at the last gasp, what kind of being his protagonist truly is. At that instant, Rubek renounces art for passion. Consequently the ending of the play is not a moment of choice between art and life, but between two kinds, two levels, of human relationship, two versions of love, two manifestations of passion, two ways, in broadest terms, of living. The contrast between them that is invited is in terms of intensity or quality. At his moment of choice, Rubek resembles Solness: he surrenders the exaltation of his calling but not the exaltation itself; *that* he must, because of his nature, carry over into his redirected passion. Out of a story about, specifically, an artist, Ibsen has woven a morality of choice between life with and life without quality, turning a particular case into a general proposition.

What I have said so far, in such (I repeat) stark terms, must seem to beg very important questions. Can it be that Irene embodies a 'virtue' and Ulfheim a 'vice', where the 'virtue' leads to death and the 'vice' to life; where the personification of 'virtue' is half-deranged and only half-alive, while the 'vice' is sensible and above all vigorous? Can it be that a play with so schematic a structure can strike us as anything more than a stiffly symbolic, coldly calculated diagram of life? To come closer to what really matters – the texture of the play, the detail out of which it is created – I want now to turn to quite a different line of approach. I want to look at the play as perhaps a would-be producer might look, at that very early stage where he is wondering how to define to himself and to his company the essential nature of the work he is about to tackle.

I think that such a person, if he approached the text with a mind uncluttered by previous interpretations, would have to decide that he must at least begin his production in a realistic style. He would naturally note the atmospheric work being done in the opening scene by the references to lack of sound, lack of life, lack of purpose in the Norwegian spa, but this in no way subverts the brilliant rendering in realistic terms of the marital comedy at the meal-table. Ibsen has caught beautifully the reality and substantiality of the characters and of the situation.

But that would not solve the producer's problem, merely define it. Perhaps in the terms: 'How the devil do I get from this scene to the scene where I have to bring on a woman who is a walking statue?'; or, in terms of language, 'How can I define a style that can encompass both the prosaic opening and the concluding lines? – how move from

MAJA: O-oh! Dear oh dear!
RUBEK: Well, Maja? What's the matter with you?
MAJA: Just listen how still it is here.

to

RUBEK: Will you follow me then, my bride of grace?
IRENE: I follow my lord and master gladly and willingly.
RUBEK: We must go through the mists first, Irene, and then . . .
IRENE: Yes, through all the mists. And then right to the peak of the tower, which shines in the sunrise?'*

Quite a problem – severe enough to tempt him to take a strong line with the play to reduce the incompatibilities; perhaps by trying to inject a symbolic elevation of style into the opening scene; or, conversely, by reducing, perhaps by ironic treatment, the elevation of the later scenes – in short, by making the whole play either naturalistic or symbolic. If he were wise, he would do neither; he would consult Ibsen with great care to see what *he* does with the problem.

I think such consultation would reveal a number of interesting little adjustments that Ibsen makes to the initial level of the play. The first comes with the introduction of the name of Rubek's masterpiece.

MAJA: . . . Besides I think it's so sad that you've lost your appetite for work.

---

* I must take responsibility for this and for the translations that follow in the remainder of this paper.

RUBEK: I've lost that too, have I?

MAJA: Just fancy, *you*, when you used to be able to work so tirelessly – all hours!

RUBEK: *Used* to, yes –

MAJA: But just as soon as you got your big masterpiece off your hands –

RUBEK (*nods thoughtfully*): 'Resurrection Day' –

MAJA: – the thing that's travelled the whole world over. That's made you so famous –

The name looks portentous on the page, invoking as it does a potential range of associations quite alien to the prosaic circumstances; perhaps it qualifies for underlining of some sort in performance, some kind of pointedly meaningful delivery. But that clearly is not Ibsen's wish. He embeds that first reference as the briefest of interjections in a steady flow of chatter from Maja. He doesn't allow time for anything to be made of it – Rubek can just manage to pop it in, and Maja's sentence rolls on. 'Resurrection Day' is Ibsen's first pebble; it causes no more than a ripple in the realistic surface.

But there *is* that ripple and Ibsen stirs it a little immediately afterwards. Not by expanding on the possible symbolic significance of 'Resurrection Day' – which could set up tension with the tone so far established – but by raising the emotional temperature. For when Rubek goes on to talk about his masterpiece he does not describe, define or interpret its significance; he merely displays strong emotion.

RUBEK: – because 'Resurrection Day' *is* a masterpiece! Or *was* to start with. No, it *is* one still. *Must, must, must* be a masterpiece!

That conveys emotion so strong that it precludes thought or analysis – Rubek can only assert with passion, giving no reasons. It is important that no part of that passion be weakened through translation or in the acting because it makes the masterpiece the focus for Rubek's vehement commitment to a certain kind of art, without turning it into anything like a symbol.

And that indicative swirl of emotion prepares for the next, which appears when Rubek talks of his other kind of art, his portrait busts.

RUBEK: . . . But at their deepest level they are decent, honest carthorses and stubborn donkeyheads and lop-eared, lowbrow dogskulls and stuffed pigheads – and feeble, brutal oxlikenesses!

Again, there should be no weakening of the indications of emotion: no insertion, in delivery, of more pauses than Ibsen provides – he provides few; no smoothing out of that congestion of adjectives and compounds. Ibsen gives us the language of pounding disgust and contempt; the outburst, following immediately on as it does from Rubek's vehemence about 'Resurrection Day', invites comparison between the two forms of art that agitate him so, the idealised and the popular, cynical kind. Without breaking the realistic surface, a potential theme – idealism versus cynicism, spiritual versus brutal? – begins to form beneath it.

Then comes the first reference to the temptation of Jesus. Surely, this time, an intrusion that calls for its solemnity to be marked in delivery by the special voice and the significant eye? But Ibsen does not invite this treatment. He introduces the reference through the most lightweight character in the play. As before, he limits its resonances by sinking it in a flow of chat.

> MAJA: . . . But do you remember what you promised me that day we came to an agreement over – over that problem –
> RUBEK (*nods*): – agreed that the two of us should get married. That was a bit hard on you, was that, Maja.
> MAJA (*continues undisturbed*): – And that I was to travel abroad with you and stay there for good – and live comfortably. – Do you remember what you promised me then?
> RUBEK (*shakes his head*): No, I honestly don't. Well, what did I promise you then?
> MAJA: You said you'd take me with you to the top of a high mountain and show me all the glory of the world.
> RUBEK (*starts*): Did I really promise that to you, too?
> MAJA (*looks at him*): Me too? Who else?
> RUBEK (*casually*): No, no, all I mean is did I promise to show you –?
> MAJA: – all the glory of the world. Yes, that's what you said. And all that glory would be mine and yours, you said.

Ibsen has conceived the dialogue in such form that 'all the glory of the world' enters the play pretty much on a par with Maja's other, prosaic, expectations – with travel and living abroad in comfort. That little coda, 'you said', somehow reduces the reference to the

level of childish petulance, re-emphasises the frivolity of the person
speaking over the implications of what she says. Furthermore, there
is the incompleteness of the reference; where, in Maja's words, is
there any glimpse of acknowledgment of the full force of the
original from which she quotes? Ibsen makes the reference enter the
play with little more force than as an unreflecting figure of speech
realistically characterising an unreflecting person.

Yet force it has. The reference clearly has a hidden significance
for Rubek. But more than that, it reinforces the precedent mention
of 'Resurrection Day' to strengthen that intimation of a scale of
values being gradually invoked that differs from anything so far
demonstrated in the mundane commerce between bored husband
and discontented wife.

And then we come to the Inspector. Not an impressive character
but one that a producer might find that he had mishandled at his
peril. He is important not as a fact-feeder but because, in a different
way, he contributes to the raising of the level of the play, not by
raising the emotional temperature, nor by establishing a focus on a
potential theme, nor by hinting at the emergence of a divergent
scale of values, but by initiating a process of excess or exaggeration.

It is there in his ponderous formalities of speech which should not
be smoothed away, in script or delivery, in the interests of
colloquialism.

INSPECTOR: A most respectful good morning, madam. – Good
morning, professor. . . . May one ask whether the lady and
gentleman have spent a peaceful night?

It would only be following the hints in the stage directions – he is
fully accoutred with hat, gloves and stick – to make him look
exaggeratedly formal too. But exaggerated in a carefully limited
way. His formalities mark him off from the other characters, yet are
justified by his job. He is exaggerated as may of us grow to be larger
(or smaller) than life through our daily occupations. To treat him as
a cameo caricature, to inflate his quirks to the point where he loses
touch with reality and floats off into the absurd, might win a few
easy laughs but would weaken him for his true function – which is to
have served as a preparation for exaggeration of a much more
significant kind.

You remember what happens. Irene appears, walks across the

stage and disappears again. Exaggeration intensified – a woman who is a walking statue. But the exaggeration has, as we have seen, been prepared for; moreover it is severely controlled. Ibsen allows a glimpse and no more; removes the startling vision (and it does startle) almost as soon as it appears, leaving us time to digest what we have seen. To eke out that first appearance of Irene, to let her linger, to provide her with any protracting business at all, would, I believe, be a great mistake.

Irene prepares the way for Ulfheim. The interaction between these two characters, in terms of the play's structure, is interesting. The brief shock of her appearance helps absorb the shock of his – another character of marked exaggeration. Together – he with his sinewy build, his hair, his obsessive brutality of manner and language – they create the impression that two characters have entered the play, whose function is to represent a value or principle rather than be, pre-eminently, realistically conceived individuals. Not that Ulfheim lacks contact with ordinary life; indeed, it is an important factor in the play's structure that he is rather more accessible, in those terms, than Irene, thus providing another rung between straight realism and pure symbolism; but that contact is the less important thing about him. Figures of symbolic significance have emerged through the surface of the play, but without abruptness. They rest upon the preliminary adaptations Ibsen has effected to the tone and atmosphere in which the play opened.

It is only after this gradual preparation that Irene fully enters the play, to substantiate the structural pattern. Ibsen has created his parallelogram, created two counsellors embodying opposed ways of living, who now embark on their respective temptations of two individualised human beings. But he has not imposed the structure as a diagram upon the living tissue of that opening scene; he has slowly elicited it from that tissue, so that the structural seems to grow out of, to remain part of, the organic. No directorial shock-tactics are needed for Irene's first sustained appearance on stage, no expressionist gimmicks. She has grown out of realism and retains roots in it. Nowhere does this show more clearly than in her language.

Ibsen had a favourite way of presenting heightened emotion – I think of it as Brandian rhetoric, because, although not exclusive to that poem nor originating in it, it suffuses *Brand* more thoroughly than any other of Ibsen's works.

In its simplest form Brandian rhetoric consists of extensive repetition of a word or phrase at the beginning of consecutive lines. One example will serve:

BRAND: How many thoughts are blunted,
       how many lively spirits stunted,
       how many manly songs affronted
       by such a rigid, crippled soul!
       How many smiles on people's faces,
       how many . . .

and so on. There are several variations: repetition in alternate lines only; repetition of two different words alternately – an a–b–a–b sequence; repetition not of the same word but of words in the same grammatical form – a sequence of lines beginning, say, with a past participle, or an imperative or an adjective; but the basic form, achieving rhetorical weight by extensively balanced repetition at the beginning of a line, remains constant.

It is a form clearly suited to verse with its well-defined line structure, and it sets up a kind of primitive secondary echo scheme to complement, and sometimes in interesting ways to counterpoint, the formal rhyme scheme at the ends of lines. Ibsen uses it from his earliest verse plays on.

But not only in his verse plays. He was soon adapting the form to prose. Just one example from *The Vikings at Helgeland*:

HJØRDIS: When Sigurd went on Viking raids and you went with
         him –
         when you heard the swords hiss in that keen contest,
         when blood smoked red on the ship's deck –
         did there not then come over you an uncontrollable
         desire to fight amongst the men;
         did you not then clothe yourself in warrior-garb and take
         a weapon in your hand?

My translation is stilted because I want to retain the form; I hope my reading showed how the prose falls into the rhetorical pattern I've been describing – with perhaps a gain in flexibility from the disappearance of formal line demarcation, of formal rhyme and rhythm. The prose does break naturally into lines; but Ibsen is able to achieve, with some ease, the modulation from the 'when Sigurd . . .' form of line to the quite different form of 'did there not' – to compose what is, in effect, a five-line 'stanza'. In prose, paradoxically, he can develop forms at least as varied as those of his verse, and, since they are used sparingly, make a stronger impact with them; but the rhetorical intent remains blatant.

Up to and including *The Pillars of Society*, Ibsen seems to think of this kind of rhetoric as a generally attributable form – does not, that is, use it to characterise a particular individual or type of individual. In *Brand*, for instance, it is spoken not only by the protagonist but by Agnes, the Doctor, Gerd and a nameless man. Nor does its use seem to indicate any of the possible negative associations of rhetoric: insincerity, inflation, duplicity, and so on. Selma uses it in *The League of Youth* and Lona in *The Pillars of Society* – figures, surely, above any suspicion of inauthenticity.

In the later modern prose plays, however, Ibsen seems to discover new possibilities in this prose rhetoric, not by new developments to its form, but by discovering new implications. He makes it suggest, not necessarily duplicity, but other more subtle kinds of falsity besides: mental arrogance, complacency, conventionality – some kind or other of incompleteness in feeling and understanding. Indeed the progress within some of the plays of the main characters can be traced by the way they exchange rhetoric for an extreme of verbal simplicity: 'No; no; no! – Yes! No; no!'; 'Now we two are one'; 'Thanks'.

What helps to make *When We Dead Awaken* so hair-raising is that Irene's language shows no traces of that favourite, diagnostic rhetoric. It would be so much easier to write her off as mad or deluded if her language were in some way suspect. But it is not. She begins her first conversation with Rubek sounding as any estranged wife might on meeting an ex-husband:

IRENE: Who was that other woman? The one you had with you – at the table there?
RUBEK: That was my – my wife.
IRENE: I see. That's good, Arnold. Then it's someone who need not concern me . . . someone you've taken after my time . . . And the child? The child is well?

There's no rhetorical *form* there; yet the *content* (to make a crude distinction) is extraordinary. I left out bits, as you will have noticed, in order to emphasise them. Irene begins by saying, '*You* are still alive, of course'. She does not say 'someone you've taken after my time' but 'after my life-time'. And after 'the child is well?' she continues: 'Our child lives on after me. In honour and glory.' She speaks in a matter-of-fact tone, yet nonetheless is revealed as a woman who thinks of herself as dead, of some thing as her child, and of that child as living in biblical splendour. It is the very tension between unrhetorical form and extraordinary content that makes Irene so disturbing. The style of utterance gives to everything she says, however bizarre, the possibility of its being in some sense true or real.

Rubek's progress in the play can be traced by reference to Irene's language. Initially it confounds him. He tries at first to reduce her to the level of prosaic understanding that he has maintained so far in the play. When, in reply to his asking where she has been, she replies, 'I went into the darkness . . . while the child stood in the light of transfiguration', all he can think of saying is the banal, 'Have you travelled about the world much?'

Irene, of course, resists this kind of reduction. The biblical content of her flat style, initiated by 'honour and glory' and 'transfiguration' (the word, in both English and Norwegian, for Jesus's transfiguration before his disciples in St Matthew's gospel) swells. She describes her incarceration in what sounds like a near paraphrase of Christ's burial and resurrection:

> IRENE: They came and bound me. Tied my arms behind my back. Then they lowered me into a tomb with iron bars in front of the opening. And with padded walls . . . so that nobody up above ground could hear the shrieks from the grave . . . But now I'm half-beginning to rise from the dead!

According to St Matthew

> When Joseph had taken the body, he wrapped it in a clean linen cloth and laid it in his own new tomb . . . and he rolled a great stone to the door of the sepulchre . . . And the angel answered and said . . . 'tell his disciples that he is risen from the dead'.

Irene's utterances become increasingly impregnated with this material until they achieve total saturation in her final words in the play.

Before long Rubek signifies his abandonment of the commonplace by beginning to use language like hers. He adopts her biblical tone: uses her word 'serve', says 'You left family and home – and followed me' – as James and John (in St Matthew) left their ship and their father and followed Jesus. Rubek's transformation is gradual. In Act I he still insists that Irene is 'alive' – the literal, commonsense word; but by early Act II he says she is 'awakened'; and when she claims that she is 'resurrected' he does not resist the idea but rather caps it with her word 'transfigured'. His language, too, swells gradually to the fullness of his last exchange with Irene.

Yet, though he can be said to use language like Irene's, Rubek's progress is that of a man re-discovering within himself a vitality that had, to all intents and purposes, been stifled. Though he comes to use the special language with some difficulty, it is clear that it was of his own original coinage. It was he, and it was in the past, before Irene's apparition, that he thought of her as 'most holy' to be 'worshipped' in thought alone to avoid his thoughts being 'profaned'.

The progress indicated by this use of language is that of a man being induced, by exhortation and temptation, to rediscover the true and cardinal sources of his own fundamental identity. In suitably moderated terms, and in a far less complex fashion, Maja's progress too can be gauged. She slips into using Ulfheim's vocabulary and sentiments under his encouragement and by doing so seems to discover her own identity.

Thus through his language, Ibsen confirms the morality pattern of his play. Two Everymen respond to the exhortations of two personified principles of living, and make their crucial choice. But he does more than that. He reinforces the feeling that this play, which moves from the realistic first scene to the symbolic elevation of the last, does so not by dislocation or imposition but by gradual adjustment that makes it appear one single organic growth that never wholly severs its roots in real experience. In the various ways I have tried, so sketchily, to describe, by subtle modulation from the realistic to the symbolic, by the gradual adumbration of a symmetry of structure and theme, by the slow and complex interaction of language, Ibsen persuades us that, however stark the final scenes, they have grown out of and refer back to living experience. A would-be producer need do nothing more, to solve the apparent problem of incompatibilities, than accept the solutions Ibsen provides for him. He may be 150 years old, but he can still teach us moderns a thing or two.

8 Ibsen and the Actors

EVERT SPRINCHORN

One of the peculiarities of the art of the theatre is that the difference between the score and the performance tends to be greater than in the other performing arts. The reason for this is that the actor is not an instrument, at least not in the sense that an oboe is. An oboe remains an oboe whatever piece is being played, but Burbage was not Betterton, Betterton was not Booth, Booth was not Barrymore, although they all played Hamlet. An oboe exists apart from the score, but Hamlet does not. The notes that an oboist plays do not give shape to an oboe, while Hamlet can be defined only by what he says and does in the script. If a dramatic part is a complicated one, it will be virtually impossible for an actor to play all the notes that make up the character. As Hamlet says, 'You would play upon me; you would seem to know my stops; you would pluck out the heart of my mystery. . . . Do you think I am easier to be played on than a pipe? Call me what instrument you will, though you can fret me, yet you cannot play upon me.' If, on the other hand, the character in the script is rather simple, a strong actor can enhance the part and add to the mystery. Hamlet remains Hamlet in spite of the number of actors who have played him, but Mathias in *The Bells* is to those who know him at all the Mathias that Henry Irving created.

The personality of an actor can brighten a dull script and transform the improbabilities of an idiotic plot into the certainties of his stage presence. All too often, however, a great actor adulterates a rich and profound script by making it serve merely as a display case for his personality. Anyone interested in great acting is not likely to object strenuously to this, since great acting is as rare as great playwriting, though literary scholars are sure to be offended. But everyone is offended when an ordinary actor turns a rich and complicated part into a theatrical stereotype. The history of acting affords a number of examples of this sort of artistic debasement.

In Sheridan's play *The School for Scandal*, Sir Peter Teazle, a man of fifty years or more, is married to an attractive girl half his age. He and she are constantly quarrelling with each other, but their quarrels are only lovers' tiffs. Sir Peter himself says, 'I think she never appears to such advantage as when she is doing everything in her power to plague me.' Sheridan sees to it that the couple stays married at the end of the play, and indicates that the flirtatious Lady Teazle will settle to a happy life with Sir Peter. When the role was originally acted, Sir Peter was represented as a vigorous man, stimulated by his wife's vivacity and high spirits. But the succeeding generations of actors portrayed Sir Peter as a decrepit old man. They turned him into a laughingstock who deserved to be ridiculed for having supposed that December could mate with May. Why the change? Because it was easier for mediocre actors to raise a laugh by acting the wheezing, shuffling, old man than to get a lasting smile by acting the middle-aged man who admires his wife's spirit and ebullience and is vigorous, charming, and solicitous enough to be loved by her.

It might be thought that dramatic characters when recreated by succeeding generations of actors would grow richer and more complicated, with subtle traits and telling acting points being invented by imaginative actors and passed on to others. But such is often not the case. One reason for this is that dramatic characters are rooted in their time, and when transported to another time they lose their fragrance and bouquet. Another reason is that great acting parts, with the enormous demands that they make, are constantly being reduced to the actor's and director's level of ability, intelligence, and knowledge. All too often actors do not do their homework properly. They settle for a characterisation that fits one of the stereotypes they are familiar with. They make Sir Peter into a silly old man because silly old men are (or were) laughable and easy to play. Such actors may make the unskilful laugh, but they cannot but make the judicious grieve.

Both these reasons help account for the prevailing lacklustre way of acting Ibsen, especially in America. There is yet another reason, however, which applies especially to Ibsen. This has to do with the stereotype to which we have reduced Ibsen. Although we hear much about his power of characterisation, the fact is that he is usually played for his ideas. We go to see an Ibsen play because for once we want an intellectual evening in the theatre or because we wish to pay tribute to a man who helped us think the right things. Though actors and actresses may regard the big Ibsen parts as living characters, they are played as if they incarnated certain social or philosophical ideas. Nora and Hedda, for example, are nowadays usually represented essentially as women trapped in a man's world, while the other characters around them exist primarily to point up the theme or dominant idea.

This approach is certainly not wrong in itself, but to stress it, as nearly everyone does, is to distort the characters and warp the real drama of the plays. To portray Nora simply as a woman who has not been able to be herself because men have always told her what to be is to ignore what it is in her that makes her realise this when thousands of other women in the same situation never came to any such realisation. Making her purely a feminist ahead of her time is like making Sir Peter merely an old man ahead of his time.

Nora has managed to stand up to this reductionist approach fairly well, but the effect on her husband Torvald Helmer has been disastrous. He has become a caricature, a cardboard husband who has no business on the stage with Nora. The people who stage *A Doll's House* obviously consider him a secondary figure, a sparring partner for Nora. It is never a real match that we see, only a demonstration of Nora's prowess as a fighter for women's rights. Within the past few years Nora has been acted by Jane Fonda, Claire Bloom, and Liv Ullmann, and everyone knows who they are. But who played Torvald opposite them? *A Doll's House* has degenerated into a vehicle for a star. Yet, ironically and fittingly, the star has not gained by this; she has lost.

For *A Doll's House* was not written as a vehicle for the actress. When it was to be staged for the first time in Stockholm, Ibsen let it be known that he wanted Gustaf Fredrikson to play the part of Torvald. Now Fredrikson was to the Stockholm stage of the 1870s what Cary Grant was to the Hollywood film of the 1930s and 1940s. Fredrikson was a matinee idol before there was such a thing, the popular star of drawing-room comedy and light melodrama, admired for his elegance and charm, and these were the qualities that Ibsen believed essential to the characterisation of Torvald.[1] The Torvalds I have seen were as charming and elegant as Punch in a puppet show. Imagine how our attitude toward the play would change if we saw the latest movie idol (assuming he had some genuine talent) as Torvald opposite a strong but not more commanding actress. Not a word of dialogue would have to be changed in order for everything to change. It would be an entirely different play.

The idea may seem unsound and impractical. Why has there not been a recent production of *A Doll's House* with a captivating Torvald? Why did not some American matinee idol play the part? Why did not Alfred Lunt play Torvald to Lynn Fontanne's Nora? Or Laurence Olivier to Vivien Leigh's Nora? Or even consider it? The reason of course is that Torvald is considered to be a thankless role. Ibsen has depicted him as a self-centred, rather insensitive man, who, when the threat of blackmail has been removed, exclaims not, '*We* are saved, Nora!' but, '*I* am saved!' If Ibsen wanted him to be charming and ingratiating, why did he make him so unsympathetic in our eyes? Again we know the reason. Ibsen was writing at a time when the sympathies of the audience would lie mainly with the husband, with Torvald, whatever sort of man he was. To give Nora a fighting chance in the struggle for the sympathies of the audience Ibsen had to darken the character of Torvald. It was in the final draft of the play that Ibsen changed '*We* are saved!' to '*I* am saved!' In the first German production of the play Nora did not leave her husband: the actress playing the part refused to represent such an immoral, unmotherly, and unnatural act on the stage. But just as Ibsen in 1879 had to give Torvald extra weight to carry in order to give Nora a fighting chance, so nowadays we must re-examine the handicaps if we wish not only to hear the words Ibsen gave his actors to speak but also to feel the tension behind them.

Once Nora and Torvald are allowed to exist as characters rather than as pieces in the campaign for the liberation of women, they become vivid and disturbingly real, and much more challenging to actors than the Nora and Torvald one ordinarily sees on stage. Torvald is after all a good father to his three children, and the attentive and ardent lover of his wife. An ambitious man with a promising career ahead of him, he is a conscientious provider who worked so hard for his family that his health collapsed. He has given Nora all the material things and all the sexual attention that any young wife could reasonably desire. He loves beautiful things, and not least his pretty wife. In fact his sense of beauty is more highly developed than hers. He plays the piano; he choreographs Nora's dance; and he does not like to see women knitting because the arm movements are ugly. And since he is fundamentally an aesthete he tends to treat Nora as a pretty object.

For years Nora appreciated all that Torvald did for her and the children as much as a normal wife would. But the change in their relationship comes about because Nora is not a normal woman. She is compulsive, highly imaginative, and very much inclined to go to extremes. She is more than a put-upon creature who resolves to fight on the barricades for the feminist cause. And Torvald is more than a selfish husband who looks upon his wife as part of his chattels personal. Like Nora, he has been formed or conditioned by social conventions and attitudes and made to play a part that by nature he is perhaps not well suited for. Bernard Shaw said that his *Candida* was a 'counterblast to Ibsen's *A Doll's House*, showing that in the real typical doll's house it is the man who is the doll.'² The truth is that the last part of Ibsen's play is the Shavian counterblast to the first part, for Torvald turns out to have been the doll all along. Torvald has regarded himself as the breadwinner in the family, the main support of his wife and children, as any decent husband would like to regard himself. When he discovers that it was Nora who sustained the family during the crucial months of his illness, it is no wonder that he is profoundly shaken. His whole concept of himself has been shattered – a concept imposed on him by society. He has unknowingly been the wife in the family. Therein lies a dramatic self-recognition that passes virtually unnoticed because all eyes are on Nora.

When Nora leaves him, she says that they might live together in a true marriage only if a great miracle occurred, a miracle of miracles. She can only mean a miracle by which Torvald would become more a wife and she more a husband. Ibsen appears to be hinting at unisexual marriage, and Torvald in the last moment of the play is willing to consider the possibility. But the change that is taking place in the apparently rigid and unyielding Torvald is never brought out in production. Only Nora is allowed to be transformed. Torvald must remain a stick-in-the-mud.

This brings us back to the question of Nora's character. Who is the real Nora – the flighty, macaroon-eating girl of the first act or the mission-minded woman of the last? There was a time when critics concerned themselves about the transformation of Nora and wondered whether her emergence as an independent spirit in the last part of the play was credible. By now, however, most actresses who undertake the role know that the strong-willed Nora is present even in the opening scenes. Only there she is playing a game, a game that has become practically second nature to her, pretending to be her husband's plaything yet knowing that he owes his very life to her. The actress must play both aspects of Nora, a task that is not difficult since Ibsen presents a Nora who at the rise of the curtain has almost made up her mind to assert her right to individuality.[3]

However, there is another aspect to the character that invariably fails to manifest itself in production because Nora is always thought of as a kind of saint, a martyr to the feminist cause, without any thought being given to what it is that makes a saint. To understand Nora fully the actress must not concern herself with the question: how could the giddy woman of the first part become the strong woman of the last act? She must ask what kind of woman is this Nora who is willing to leave her husband and children, not for another man, mind you, but in order to find out how much validity there is in the ideas that have been inculcated in her since she was a child. There were any number of women in Ibsen's time who had greater cause to rebel, women with cruel and abusive husbands, women without any children to bind them to home and husband, women without the comforts of a middle-class house. What is there in Nora, a woman who has all a woman of her time – and perhaps of our time – could reasonably hope for, that makes her see the injustice of a world that everyone else accepts, and rebel against it? What is it that sets her apart from all the other women who meekly accepted their lot even when their lot was much worse than Nora's?[4]

It is obvious that Ibsen has carefully and deliberately seen to it that Nora does not have the ordinary reasons for leaving her husband. Apparently she leaves Torvald because he does not live up to her ideal. All along she has imagined that Torvald is a kind of romantic hero, as willing to make sacrifices as she is. When, instead of offering to sacrifice his name and reputation for her sake, he upbraids her as an unprincipled woman, she realises she has been living with a man she does not really know. The man she thought she had married was the product of her romantic imagination. As a man of his times Torvald is partly responsible for fostering these romantic notions about male and female roles, notions that are as flattering to him as they are impossible for him to live up to.

Let me indicate very quickly what Ibsen lets us learn about Nora. She has been dominated by men all her life, her mother having died when Nora was very young. As a child she was completely under the spell of her father, and as a wife she has been completely under the spell of her husband. She has always been protected, cared for, and perhaps spoiled. This has made her egocentric, and indifferent to the sufferings of others. She knew of the plight of her good friend Christine but never bothered to communicate with her. She flirts cruelly with Dr Rank and toys with his deep affection for her, drawing him on to find out how strong her hold over him actually is. Most revealing of all is the way she went about saving her husband. She was not compelled to borrow from a stranger and forge her father's signature on a promissory note. She could have turned to friends of her husband for the necessary money; any other woman would have done so. But Nora knew that if she turned to one of Torvald's friends for help, she would have had to share her role of saviour with someone else. By borrowing from a stranger and forging her father's signature, she sees herself as sparing the sufferings of two people, her husband who is ill and her father who is dying. Thus the doll becomes the rescuer of the men who made her a doll. She revels in the role of saviour, proving herself ultimately superior to her husband, secretly enjoying the reversal of roles, and knowing that from now on Torvald will always and inescapably be in her debt. In her imagination she foresees the time when, growing old and less attractive to Torvald, she can reveal how she saved him. It is her insurance policy against the future. The 'most wonderful thing of all' of which she speaks is the gratitude toward her that Torvald must feel when he eventually learns the truth. That moment is suddenly brought from the distant future into the present when Krogstad, from whom she borrowed the money, threatens to expose her as a criminal. Responding hysterically to this threat, she lets her thoughts rush ahead. If she viewed her situation calmly, she would realise that no serious crime had been committed; the only threat is to Torvald's reputation. Now she imagines Torvald interceding on her behalf, taking her crime on his shoulders, behaving as the men in her life have always done, protecting her, and thereby being superior to her. But this time it will be different. She will forestall Torvald, deny his guilt to the world, and then drown herself. Dying for Torvald's sake, she will forever remain superior to him.

In this brilliant analysis, which I have extracted from a probing commentary written by a psychiatrist in 1907, we have the real Nora.[5] Here we see what makes the martyr and feminist who slams the door on husband and children. The actress who endeavours to portray Nora in all her complexity must centre her efforts not on the last scene, the remarkable discussion between the self-righteous husband and the disillusioned wife, a scene that plays itself, but on the tarantella scene that Ibsen intended as the climax of the drama and that brings the curtain down on the second act. In her Italian costume, which is associated with the journey to the south that saved her husband's life, Nora is still the plaything of her husband. But the frenetic dance that she performs and that Torvald feels compelled to interrupt is in her mind a sacrificial dance. In thirty-one hours she will throw herself into the river for her husband's sake. The dancing doll will become the human martyr, and this time not in secret. In that hysterical tarantella the two sides of Nora reveal themselves simultaneously. (The symbolism of the dance is equally appropriate whether the tarantella is thought of as the dance caused by the bite of the tarantula or as the dance meant to drive the spider's poison from the victim's system.)

The reverse side of the noble feminist is what one does not see on stage. But any actress who wants to represent the woman Ibsen created must act the double intention, must act both Noras, the Nora who is deceitful yet honest, theatrical yet sincere, insensitive and inconsiderate yet willing to give her life for her husband, a woman who is cunning enough to know that she is only playing a game for his benefit, only pretending to be a doll, yet who keeps in her mind a naive, romantic view of him as hero, a woman who sees herself as so much in debt to the male sex that the only possible way she can repay the debt is to give her own life, a woman whose whole world crumbles into dust when she discovers that the one thing she thought was real in it, her husband, proves to be a doll also. What we do see on stage is only, at best, half of this Nora, half of the richest, most complex female character that any dramatist had created since Shakespeare's time.

It has often been said that Chekhov's characters are as complicated as living people, and his plays are frequently compared to icebergs. The script, the printed text, is only the tip of the iceberg. In order to portray a Chekhov character the actor must create from the one-tenth of the character that is plainly visible the nine-tenths that lie submerged. So acting students write imaginary biographies of these characters, improvise new scenes for them, and invent all sorts of business to give the fullest sense of reality to Chekhov's people. Every effort is made to endow these fictional figures with flesh and blood, to dissociate them from abstract ideas, to see to it that they do not become caricatures. In contrast, every effort is made, often unconsciously, to shape Ibsen's creations as the embodiments of ideas. The result has been harmful to both

dramatists. Chekhov's characters have been made more complicated than they really are, and Ibsen's less so. Chekhov
concerned himself mostly with simple, ordinary people, whose
aspirations are relatively modest, and who are not divided against
themselves. 'Let us be just as simple and complex as life itself is', said
Chekhov. 'People sit down to dine and their happiness is made or
destroyed.' His characters are what they seem to be. In portraying
them on stage the actor looks for the 'spine' of the character and
fleshes it out with true-to-life touches. Of Madame Ranevskaya, one
of the choicest roles in the Chekhov canon, Chekhov himself said, 'It
is not difficult to play [her]; only one has to find the right key from
the very beginning; one has to find a smile and a way of laughing;
one must be able to dress.'[6] The major characters in Ibsen – Nora,
Hedda, Mrs Alving, Torvald, Gregers, Solness, Allmers – cannot
be represented in this simple, direct way, though that is the way they
are usually represented. Chekhov's characters are meant to be
ordinary people, not very neurotic, not very disturbed. Madame
Ranevskaya, a woman with a past, and with a lover waiting for her
in Paris, is not nearly as troubled by her conscience as her
counterpart in Ibsen would be. For one sentimental moment she
speaks of her sins, but she quickly puts the past out of her mind and
journeys back to Paris. It is not a question of Chekhov's having less
insight into human nature than Ibsen; it is a question of different
kinds of people. Ibsen dealt with extremists, people with divided
souls. Chekhov did not, except in the case of Constantine Treplev,
the failed writer who commits suicide. He belongs in Ibsen, just as
Hjalmar Ekdal, who has no understanding of extremists, would be
right at home among Chekhov's characters. Chekhov's view of the
world was essentially comic; Ibsen's essentially tragic. Chekhov's
people take what the world offers; Ibsen's heroes want more than
the world could possibly provide.

Gregers Werle in *The Wild Duck* is a uniquely Ibsenian creation,
an idealist tormented by guilt, imposing himself where he is not
wanted, and wreaking havoc where he thought he was bringing
peace and harmony. Everyone knows that in writing *The Wild Duck*
Ibsen was repudiating his former crusading self, and that in
Gregers he wished to show the harm caused by a zealot bent on
making the world live up to his idea of perfection. Even actors know
this, or find it out soon enough, and inevitably they end up
portraying a Gregers who fits this preconception of the part. And
sure enough, everything the actor finds in the script appears to fit

this preconception. Gregers is harmful: he blunders into the happy Ekdal home and destroys it. His influence is pernicious: little Hedwig commits suicide because of his mad talk. He is a fool: he idolises Hjalmar Ekdal, though it is obvious to every other adult in the play that he is a self-indulgent, lazy, pampered egotist. And to make certain that the audience recognises Gregers from the first moment as a hostile figure, Ibsen has made him repulsive in appearance, ugly of feature and physically clumsy. The portrait verges on caricature.

But suppose we were to examine Gregers without any preconceptions about Ibsen's ideas. We would see all that I have mentioned, but we would see much else besides. We would see a man who had an unhappy childhood, brought up in a house in which mother and father had nothing in common, who saw hate grow between his parents, saw his mother become a hopeless alcoholic, and, seeing his mother decline, came to hate his father. When he was an adolescent, his closest friend was Hjalmar Ekdal, a cheerful, handsome young man, coddled by the two aunts who reared him and loved by a father who shared with his boy many of the pleasures of life, taking the boy out hunting with him, for example; and those happy days in the forest are the ones father and son relive in their make-believe forest in the garret. Hjalmar had everything that Gregers dreamed of having. And then, when they were both about twenty years old, there occurred the business scandal that ruined the Ekdal family. His father's part in this affair made Gregers detest him all the more, and because of his own silence when his word might have helped the Ekdals, Gregers has ever since been weighed down with the burden of guilt. In trying to lighten that burden he became a crusader, a fanatic crying out to all and sundry, 'Ye shall know the truth and the truth shall make you free', believing that the cure his damaged soul needed must be good for all souls. Having been silent and untruthful at a crucial moment, he has since resolved to speak the truth, convinced that the momentary pain the truth may cost is as nothing compared to the years of anguish he has suffered for shirking the truth. This is the man who comes to the home of Hjalmar Ekdal and finds a god-given opportunity to redeem his own sin against the Ekdal family by telling Hjalmar, the idol of his youth, the truth about Hjalmar's wife and her involvement with old Werle. Monomaniacal and compulsive about the truth, especially about a truth that will allow him to atone for his silence years ago by exposing his father now as he should have exposed him then,

Gregers never stops to consider the alternatives. He judges the situation from his own experience. The other side of the question is like the other side of the moon to him. He has never known the kind of happiness that comes when affection and fellow-feeling palliate the truth and make it bearable. His parents had no love for him. He will never be a husband or a father, and he knows it. He is not only psychically ill; he is also physically ill, suffering from some kind of nervous disease. At the end of the play, seeing that Hedwig has committed suicide, he is seized with convulsions ('*krampaktige rykninger*').

All this may not make Gregers appealing, but it does help us to understand him, and understanding is not too far removed from sympathy. However, there is yet another quality in him that is slighted by the actors. Gregers is always presented as oblivious to the feelings of others. He is as gauche emotionally as he is physically. Yet it is Gregers who of all the people in the drama strikes the deepest chords in the child Hedwig. In the most haunting scene in the play Gregers penetrates Hedwig's secret world, speaks of the 'briny depths of the sea', and forges a bond with her that has the strength of absolute faith. She is decidedly the most sympathetic and endearing person in the play. She senses something in Gregers that the others do not. In order to make the outcome convincing what she senses in him must be sensed by the audience, too. That is why it is incumbent on the actor to elevate Gregers in this scene far beyond the usual conception of him as a crazy, demented fool, which is how Dr Relling sees him, and to make him, at least for the moment, a man of spiritual insight whose concerns are with man's highest endeavours. Dr Relling, who believes in the necessity of the life-lie, the need that people have for illusions about themselves, may understand ordinary mortals, but it is Gregers who understands extraordinary beings.

In the scene with Hedwig, Gregers is not some demon casting an evil spell on the child. The scene is infused with all the pain and anguish that Gregers has experienced in life, all his loneliness, and with all the special kind of understanding that he has gained from the unhappiness that he has known. Unless this positive aspect of Gregers is brought out by the actor, something vital to the play will be lost. The scene with Hedwig constitutes the preparation for Hedwig's drastic act at the end of the play. If Gregers is not made fascinating in the way that prophets are fascinating, the workings of Hedwig's mind will be only half comprehensible. If Gregers is seen by the audience only as Dr Relling sees him, and that is the usual way of looking at him, *The Wild Duck* dwindles into a thesis play, Relling is reduced to being the author's mouthpiece, and Gregers appears as only the husk of a living person.

Because actors and directors have failed to explore the depths of Ibsen's characters, we are seeing only a part of the plays that Ibsen wrote, and perhaps only a part of the plays that our grandparents saw. Though there has been a general improvement in acting, our actors and directors have lost some of the insight and instinctive understanding that an earlier generation may have had, since they were closer in time and spirit to the original figures. To regain that lost ground and advance beyond it, it is necessary to look at these characters freshly and to put into the stage representation of them all the apparent inconsistencies, all the convolutions of thought, all the layers of emotional life that lie in the scripts of the plays. Actors now give us the emerging feminist in Nora and the crazy idealist in Gregers. But how much more interesting these characters would be, and how much more controversial and stimulating the plays would become if the actors presented not only the feminist in Nora but also the hysterical woman who is willing to leave husband and children in order to find out whether she alone or the whole world is right; not only the obsessed truth-seeker in Gregers but also the wretchedly unhappy man who can only give meaning to his own life by vicariously living Hjalmar's. Ideas are an essential element in Ibsen's plays, but ideas are made by people and transmitted by people. 'The actor's business', said Bernard Shaw in reviewing one of Ibsen's plays, 'is not to supply an idea with a sounding board, but with a credible, simple, and natural human being to utter it when its time comes and not before.'[7]

And ultimately people are more complex and controversial than ideas. 'Why is there so much concern about what my plays mean?' asked Ibsen. 'We all act and write under the influence of some idea or other. The question is: have I succeeded in creating a good drama with living persons?'[8] He usually succeeded, but all too often the actors have not.

NOTES

1. See Ibsen's letter to the Royal Theatre, Stockholm, 1 October 1879, in *Ibsens brevväxling med Dramatiska teatern*, ed. Stig Torsslow (Stockholm, 1973), p. 22.

2. Letter to Beverley Baxter, in the *Evening Standard*, London, 30 November 1944; reprinted in *A Casebook on Candida*, ed. Stephen S. Stanton (New York, 1962), p. 158.

3. See Henry Rose, *Henrik Ibsen: Poet, Mystic and Moralist* (London, 1913), p. 41.

4. Magdalene Thoresen, the step-mother of Ibsen's wife, regarded Nora as a kind of female Jesus. (Letter to Frederikka Limnell, 17 February 1880, in Lotten Dahlgren, *Lyran* (Stockholm, 1913), p. 316.

5. Erich Wulffen, *Ibsens Nora vor dem Strafrichter und Psychiater* (Halle, 1907). The essay on Nora by Hermann J. Weigand in his *The Modern Ibsen* (New York, 1925), is equally perceptive. On Nora as definitely the hysterical type, who lies pathologically, suppresses her emotions, and suffers from bad traits inherited from her father, see Dr Robert Geyer, *Etude médico-psychologique sur le théâtre d'Ibsen* (Paris, 1902), pp. 37–39.

6. Letter to Olga Knipper, 25 October 1903.

7. Shaw, *Our Theatres in the Nineties* (Standard Edition, London, 1932), III, p. 128.

8. Le Comte Prozor, Introduction to *Le Petit Eyolf* (Paris, 1895), p. xxv. Also in Prozor, 'Ibsen's "Lille Eyolf,"' *Ord och Bild*, IV (1895), p. 370.

9 The Structured World of Ibsen's Late Dramas

JAMES McFARLANE

I take as my starting point a proposition I have recently made in another context,[1] and which I take leave to re-state here in approximate phrases: that as one follows Ibsen's dramatic output from the late 1870s, through the 1880s and into the 1890s, one becomes aware that what increasingly preoccupied him was a sense of the world as an arena of relationships and of meta-relationships, i.e. the relationship between relationships.

It is important (for the avoidance of later misunderstanding) that I emphasise that I say 'increasingly' and not 'exclusively'. For a dramatist whose early fascination for the nature of Selfhood had in its time been so consuming, it is unrealistic to suppose that problems of individual identity would ever totally cease to engage his attention. I speak essentially of relative change and suggest that the emphasis in the later dramas is less on characters or people for what they *are* than on what passes between them, on what it is that holds them together in tension or forces them apart, on the dynamics of situations where ties are made and broken, where mutual support is awarded or denied, where attractions and repulsions are exerted. The world of these later dramas is only imperfectly defined if it is seen primarily as a world of separate individuals, each with his or her own personal aspirations and frustrations, with his or her circle of friends, associates, confidants or enemies, as a community of egocentric wills moving each in its own personal space, with all the contingent jostlings, collisions and fusions that follow from this.

Rather it declares itself as a system of complex multiple relationships, where sets of interrelated entities are held from moment to moment in a dynamic of rarely more than temporary and uneasy stability, where the dominant factor is the force (in something like the physicist's sense) exerted by one body upon another, by one mind upon another, and where the varying direction and magnitude of these forces determine the changing configuration of the entire system. For in the dramatic situation (as in life) none of the linear relationships is in itself a discrete, exclusive thing, divorced from other contingent relationships. The result then is that attention is inevitably drawn to the problem of how these relationships themselves relate to each other, how an integrated system of sets – triangular, quadrilateral, or more elaborately polygonal – forms itself out of their mutual interdependence. The end product is then a lattice of relationships, which ultimately achieves some greater or lesser degree of resolution, which is shifting or fluid as in life, yet which from moment to moment enjoys a temporary stability. I would then argue that it is not the precise location in absolute terms of the separate *points*, not their specific coordinates at any one time, that deserves our best attention, but rather the emotional trigonometry of their relative dispositions and the path of their movements relative to each other within the time dimension of the dramatic action.

To put it abstractly (and thus, in this present company, provocatively): in the lattice of conjoined points A, B, C, D . . . (which is my model of the world of the late dramas) we should be less concerned to 'place' A, B, C, D . . . than we should be to examine the linking relationships AB, BC, CD, AC, BD . . . Moreover, we should be alertly aware that within the triangle ABC (for example), the determination of the relationship AB is to a very large extent dependent upon a successful analysis of the relationship between the two relationships BC and AC. But then again, the relationship AB is also to a significant degree determined by its role within the further triangle ABD, in which it is then the relationship between BD and AD (the included angle, as it were) which helps to determine the definition. And so on, by further triangulation, throughout the system.

It is then on the basis of such a model that these later dramas explore the complex interactions, the interdependencies, the shifts and dislocations, the endless conjoining and disjoining of multiple relationships which, though individually often deceptively simple and linear, combine into chains and patterns of daunting elaboration and subtlety. Each discrete relationship is discovered imposing its own peculiar imperatives, raising its own inhibitions, exerting its own special kind of attraction and compulsion. Within this containing structure of inter-latticed relationships, this plexus of blood ties and family ties, of parenthood and childhood, of sex and marriage, of youth and age, the inhabitants of the Ibsenist world are subjected to close and intense scrutiny as they stumble in agonised pursuit of happiness and fulfilment.

But what – it needs to be asked – is the nature of these compulsions, these relational imperatives, in general terms? Possibly the most obvious, certainly the most accessible (though not necessarily the most imperious) of the determining relationships in these plays are those of the kinship systems there established, with their codified obligations and duties. They trace an elaborate geometry, an intricate interweaving of ties parental and filial, of sibling and other blood relationships, of affiliate and affinal connections of astonishing variety. Family and kinship obligations are seen occupying a wide band on the spectrum of '*pligt*', that larger concept of duty which emerges as one of the dominating forces in these later dramas, exacting from the individual – under pain of 'guilt' – the kind of conduct which convention or tradition or society's expectations impose on those who are caught up in such webs of conflicting and competing obligations.

To enumerate the various complex blood-relationships, the socio-legal relationships and the sexual relationships in these late plays is to enter upon a formidable catalogue. Prominent is the emphasis given to the obligations and aspirations of parenthood: the ambitions and duties of fatherhood (literal as well as metaphorical) are prominent in the careers of Allmers, Borkman and Rubek; the torments and rewards of motherhood (as natural mother, step-mother, foster-mother, adoptive mother, or surrogate mother) are repeatedly appealed to by Rita, Gunhild, Ella and Irene as things of decisive importance in the business of living. Then comes the extensive range of sibling relationships in these plays. They, along with blood ties and affinal ties of a more tenuous kind, function as a further range of determinants in directing individual conduct. These are augmented by the wide variety of sexual relationships which run in parallel with these: marital, pre-marital and extra-marital, consummated and unconsummated, promiscuous and abstinent, invited and withheld, sensualised and sublimated, overt and suppressed, deviant and incipiently incestuous. What then uncompromisingly engages our attention is how these multifarious relationships – kinship and sexual – themselves relate to each other; how, in particular contexts, they establish a hierarchy of compul-

sions, determine individual priorities, assert a pattern of su-
premacies

The moment has surely arrived when you will wish me to leave the
arena of theoretical generalisation, turn my back on trigonomet-
rical abstractions, and consider an aspect of the concrete reality of
these late plays. Let me then turn to *Little Eyolf*, the world of which is
initially presented as an apparently established and reasonably
stable though admittedly complex system of personal relationships – a world which is then subjected to abrupt and profound re-
alignment and readjustment through the agency of catastrophe and
revelation.

The initial situational system is swiftly and economically defined
in the opening scenes as one involving four central characters
(Alfred, Rita, Asta and Eyolf) and two peripheral ones (Borgheim
and the Rat-wife), held in a lattice of interlocking and overlapping
relationships. The lattice conspicuously embodies the duties of
motherhood and fatherhood, the connubial obligations of husband
and wife, the loyalties and affections of putative siblings, and sexual
attraction in a variety of forms: insistent, fearful, suppressed,
deviant and taboo'd. Alfred has three competing roles: husband,
father, and half-brother. Rita is wife, mother, and (half) sister-in-
law. Asta is half-sister, (half) sister-in-law, and (half) aunt – a role
which in the particular circumstances also invites her to act as
usurpative mother. As for Eyolf, he is son (with father-directed and
mother-directed loyalties) as well as (half) nephew. Into this tight
and relatively complex system of parental, affinal, matrimonial and
sexual links, of overlapping and competing attractions and repulsions, duties and desires, Borgheim and the Rat-wife are then
fatefully introduced as further augmentation of the pattern of
relationships.

Diagrammatically this might be represented in a mathematical
figure where

$$M = \text{Man, or Alfred Allmers}$$
$$W = \text{Woman, or Rita Allmers}$$
$$S = \text{Sister, or Asta Allmers}$$
$$C = \text{Child, or Little Eyolf}$$
$$B = \text{Borgheim}$$
$$R = \text{Rat-wife.}$$

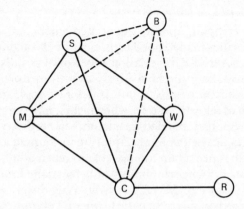

At the heart of this system (or, in more orthodox terms, central to the play) is the line MW, the Man-Woman (indeed the husband-wife) relationship; and from the play's opening moments one begins to register the signs that betray something of the nature of that relationship. But it very soon becomes evident that it is impossible satisfactorily to define this Man-Woman (sexual/connubial) relationship without first registering the nature of the two parental relationships towards the child Eyolf, i.e. the father-child and the mother-child bonds. In other words, and in the language of abstractions, a significant constituent of the relationship link MW can only be adequately defined by first determining the nature of the MC (i.e. Alfred-Eyolf) and the WC (i.e. Rita-Eyolf) relationships within the general triangle MWC.

Immediately then the complex subtlety of the overall relationship pattern begins to announce itself:

(a) Alfred declares his intention of devoting himself to the child; or, in other words, to put his wife in a subordinate position to the son. Significantly, he is concerned on his return from a longish absence more with the child's digestion than with his wife's allurements.

(b) Rita states categorically that she puts motherhood second to wifehood, and declares she will not tolerate a situation where her child is a successful claimant (in rivalry with her) for her husband's attention and affection.

(c) The past history of the child's affliction is revealed, whereby it is intimated that sexual relations between man and wife are fraught with crippling, paralysing consequences.

It is then further made abundantly clear by the action of the play that this MW (Alfred-Rita) relationship cannot be fully understood except by also taking the half-sisterly as well as the half-sister-in-lawly relationship into full account. It is, for example, revealed that Alfred, who had felt only 'terror' when he first met the girl Rita who became his wife, had married for money – not selfishly for himself, but in order to secure the financial future for himself and his sister. In other words, once again it is possible to reach a full understanding of the husband-wife relationship only by taking into account the triangular relationship MWS, i.e. Man-Wife-Sister.

Superimposed on this is then the further revelation that the Man-Sister relationship is a good deal more complex than might at first sight have been assumed; and it becomes clear that it can be fully understood only by examining the triangle MSC, i.e. the triangular links that hold together Man-Sister-Child. One is made to record how the girl Asta, the half-sister, had when they were younger dressed up in boy's clothes to please her brother; how on such occasions he had given her the name Eyolf; and how, when his own son was born, he had baptised him by the fateful name Eyolf.

Thus is the attention directed to the triangle SWC, to the Sister-Wife-Child plexus, within which it is revealed that Asta had been more of a 'mother' to Eyolf than had Rita, the natural mother and wife. In consequence of which, Rita sees Asta as both a rival for her son's affection and as a threat to her matrimonial happiness.

Then to admit Borgheim into the system (as indeed we must) necessarily introduces other relational links:

(a) He is (initially, very nearly) engaged to Asta.

(b) He is, because he buys Eyolf a bow and arrows and announces that he is going to teach him how to swim, a kind of surrogate 'father' to him, in consequence of which the triangle BSC (i.e. Borgheim-Asta-Eyolf) distortingly mirrors the *real* father-mother-child relationship.

(c) Rita, when seeking to put sexual pressure on Alfred, threatens to run off with Borgheim, and effectively establishes two further dynamic triangular relationships, namely MWB (i.e. Alfred-Rita-Borgheim) and WSB (i.e. Rita-Asta-Borgheim).

So one might go on, adding further detail, to thicken up the lattice of relationships which hold together these individual characters in unstable tension. The point I am endeavouring to make is that this is a coherent relational system, held together in equilibrium by its own inherent forces, within which any one part can be properly defined and understood only by relating it to the other parts in the whole.

Then two things happen within the drama to disrupt the uneasy equilibrium: (a) the Rat-wife exerts her mysterious and sinister attractive power on the child, whereby the child suffers death by drowning, and in consequence immediately disturbs the parental/connubial relationship; and (b) the incest taboo in force between Alfred and Asta is removed by the revelation that they have no natural (as distinct from legal) parents in common, a revelation which also has a complex knock-on effect throughout the entire relational system. Whereupon the drama goes on to trace the consequential violent re-adjustments imposed on the original lattice of relationships by these sudden incursions of fateful event.

I have of course greatly coarsened and simplified what happens in the play: there is much more contributory and persuasive detail, and a much greater subtlety of definitive motivation. But one of these developments neatly exemplifies what I began by suggesting: when it is discovered that Alfred and Asta are not in fact half-siblings, it is incontrovertibly clear that it is the *relationship*, and not them, which has changed. As individuals, they remain 'the same' as before; nothing in their own intrinsic nature has altered, but by this significant revelation, not only is the essential relationship between them changed, but the change is transmitted throughout the entire system to affect the remotest extremities of it.

There is however one further feature of Ibsen's world which needs constantly to be borne in mind when analysing the mechanics of causation in it: and that is that it is a thoroughly deceptive world. Deceit is endemic; self-deception commonplace; witnesses, particularly where their own motives and conduct are concerned, are frequently unreliable; dissimulation becomes a way of life. And it is absolutely crucial to realise that one must constantly beware of accepting the characters and their own version of events merely at face value.

One remarks in these dramas a high incidence of those who, consciously or unconsciously, rationalise their own conduct in deceptive terms, who are quick to designate as duty or as necessity a course of action which at the deeper level is dictated by essentially selfish motives, who devise plausible altruisms in order to escape from situations which either they find distasteful or in which they sense themselves to be inadequate. As a recent Norwegian critic[2] has put it: Ibsen's lifelong preoccupation with the nature of human frailty and error and self-deception makes his work particularly susceptible to misreading. Ibsen's characters *lie*, even if only in the sense that we all lie, all give subjectively coloured accounts of past events and present, all seek to assert ourselves or protect ourselves, to impress or manipulate others. Only by reading Ibsen's works *suspiciously* (it is suggested) does one avoid the traps of superficial (and thus false) interpretation. Ibsen is concerned to reveal the *secret* springs of human conduct; and the chief factor at work in the communication of this is the dramatist's compositional, structural skill.

If then, in the light of this recognition, one asks the crucial question – 'How does one set about eliciting the true 'meaning' of these plays?' – I would first have to reply evasively (with I. A. Richards) that anyone who lets himself in for a public discussion of 'meaning' is already half-way to delirium. Nevertheless, I have said enough to indicate that the 'meaning' of these plays is most rewardingly approached through a study of their *structure*, via a wary and indeed suspicious examination of the shifts and dislocations which stressful event wreaks on their world of latticed relationships. Such an approach clearly requires that one works with some kind of structuralist semantic – 'structuralist', that is, with a small initial 's'. This is simply to re-affirm that for a dramatist to structure a dynamic situation in the dramatic mode is in itself to communicate a meaning; and the more skilful and subtle and resolved the changing balances of that situation, the more subtle the communication, the greater the semantic enrichment.

And when we ask what is then the role of language in this structuralist semantic, we need to remind ourselves that, within this integrated system of signs and signals, words are significant chiefly as they relate to, as they complement, the structured situation. Once again I have recourse to an idea from I. A. Richards which, though by now elderly, is still capable of enormous elucidatory power: his notion that, within the standard literary context, 'the meaning of a word is the missing part of its context.' To extend this to the dramatic situation is but a short step, yielding the proposition that the meaning of the words is the missing part of the dramatic context, the dramatically structured situation. The force and power of any selected utterance can then be seen relating to the eloquence of the created situation of which it is the final consummating element, the detonating factor that completes and primes the emotively explosive device, the releasing agent in a geometry of tension.

The verbal component (as we have frequently been reminded in this conference) can in *itself* be a seemingly insignificant thing: '*Se paa barnet*' ('Look at the child'); '*Og saa kom det*' ('And then it happened'). My contention is that to isolate these utterances and examine them for some kind of intrinsic worth, for orthodox 'poetic' or rhetorical qualities, is misplaced endeavour. Since it derives its power to move almost wholly from its context of situation, the *verbal* element can not only very effectively be flat, bleak, prosaic, but it can even, in appropriate circumstances, be almost entirely eliminated from the composition of the dramatic situation – a situation which nevertheless continues to communicate by way of its own kind of eloquence. Drama continues, as it has always done, to mount raids on the inarticulate; but, in the modern age particularly, it is largely through the very device of inarticulation. Conspicuously evident in today's drama is a reduced dependence on the purely unsupported resources of words, a preoccupation with the verbally understated, the throw-away, the tangential, the inconsequential, a penetration into areas of human experience into which simple verbalisation cannot by itself enter. As Pinter put it in 1960:

> A character on stage who can present no convincing argument or information as to his past experience, his present behaviour or his aspirations nor give a complete analysis of his motives is as legitimate and as worthy of attention as one who, alarmingly, can do all these things. The more acute the experience, the less articulate its expression.

It is a line of thinking that goes straight back to the final moments of *Ghosts*, to a created situation where conventional language has been almost completely pared away, where words fail and speech becomes an idiot's babble and a mother's cry of pain and irresolution and where, in the overall interdependence of parts in the dramatic mode, the role of verbalisation is reduced almost to vanishing point, and the structured situation is all.

NOTES

1. This paper draws in some measure on certain ideas (and indeed on certain phrases) I first put forward in my Introduction to volume 8 of *The Oxford Ibsen* (London, 1977), and attempts to follow them through further.
2. Jørgen Haugen, *Henrik Ibsens metode* (Copenhagen, 1977).

Index